Divine Prayers for Despairing Parents

Words to Pray When You Don't Know What to Say

SUSANNE SCHEPPMANN

D0802127

New Hope® Publishers
P. O. Box 12065
Birmingham, AL 35202-2065
www.newhopepublishers.com

New Hope Publishers is a division of WMU®.

Library of Congress Cataloging-in-Publication Data

Scheppmann, Susanne, 1954-
  Divine prayers for despairing parents : words to pray when you don't know what to say / Susanne Scheppmann.
    p. cm.
  Includes index.
  ISBN-13: 978-1-59669-206-0 (sc)
  ISBN-10: 1-59669-206-5 (sc)
  1. Parents--Prayers and devotions. I. Title.
  BV4845.S34 2009
  242'.845--dc22
                        2008041739

ISBN-10: 1-59669-206-5
ISBN-13: 978-1-59669-206-0

N084132 • 0209 • 4M1

Dedication

For the Parent in Despair: Trust the Divine

Jesus continued: "There was a man who had two sons. The younger one said to his father, 'Father, give me my share of the estate.' So he divided his property between them.

"Not long after that, the younger son got together all he had, set off for a distant country and there squandered his wealth in wild living. After he had spent everything, there was a severe famine in that whole country, and he began to be in need. So he went and hired himself out to a citizen of that country, who sent him to his fields to feed pigs. He longed to fill his stomach with the pods that the pigs were eating, but no one gave him anything.

"When he came to his senses, he said, 'How many of my father's hired men have food to spare, and here I am starving to death! I will set out and go back to my father and say to him: Father, I have sinned against heaven and against you. I am no longer worthy to be called your son; make me like one of your hired men.' So he got up and went to his father.

"But while he was still a long way off, his father saw him and was filled with compassion for him; he ran to his son, threw his arms around him and kissed him.

"The son said to him, 'Father, I have sinned against heaven and against you. I am no longer worthy to be called your son."

"But the father said to his servants, 'Quick! Bring the best robe and put it on him. Put a ring on his finger and sandals on his feet. Bring the fattened calf and kill it. Let's have a feast and celebrate. For this son of mine was dead and is alive again; he was lost and is found.' So they began to celebrate."

—Luke 15:11–24

Table of Contents

Acknowledgments

With special thanks:

To my husband, Mark,
who never doubted this book would come to fruition.

To Andrea Mullins, who believed in this book —
not once, but twice.

To Joyce Dinkins,
whose godly encouragement perfected this work of my heart.

To Margaret Traudt, a sister of my heart
for her love of words and knowledge of grammar.

Before You Read

"You will never understand the pain of my heart until you're a mom," I said to my son.

"I'll never be a mom," he retorted.

"Ah, my point exactly. You will never understand how I feel right now," I said as my tears puddled on the brown tile floor.

This conversation with my son took place several years ago. He may never understand, but every parent will. Raising children brings joy and heartache. I, too, caused my parents much heartache, by wandering away from the faith.

Divine Prayers for Despairing Parents is written from my various experiences: as a prodigal child, as a mother of three children, and as a listener who has heard stories from hundreds of moms who have shared their heart's pain over a wayward child.

The devotions are anecdotal in nature. Several are derived from my own experiences as that of a rebellious young woman—my thoughts, intentions, and faulty rationale. Many stories are based on my experiences and emotions as the mother of an errant child. Others are based on the real-life stories of countless friends and other women whom I have ministered to for more than decade.

In some of the devotions, I have changed gender references—*she* to *he* and vice versa—to help protect some of the children's identities, both the innocent and the guilty.

My intent is for this book to remind us that, when anxiety overwhelms us, when scorching pain sears our heart, and when the darkness of the unknown threatens to engulf us, we can call to Jesus, the Light of the world. He hears our prayers and His Word never comes back without results.

"So is my word that goes out from my mouth: It will not return to me empty, but will accomplish what I desire and achieve the purpose for which I sent it."
—Isaiah 55:11

How to Use the Devotions

Divine Prayers for Despairing Parents is written and designed to aid you in praying for your child. Each devotional prayer has three sections geared to help relieve your personal pain and to help you pray for your child:

- An anecdotal devotion to launch your heart, mind, and soul into believing God for His love of your child and yourself
- A Scripture passage to read and meditate on
- A prayer that is a paraphrase of the Scripture passage, with blanks for you to insert your child's name to make it a personal prayer for your child

The book is divided into 18 sections that each have a particular focus. You may read and pray through *Divine Prayers for Despairing Parents* in several different ways:

- Read and pray from the beginning to end.
- Choose a particular section that will aid you in praying for your child.
- Spontaneously choose prayers from day to day as God guides you.

1

Whispers of Hope

Silent Night

I waited for the phone to ring. The blackness of the night began to smother me as I listened in hope for the front door to open and close. Nothing. Silence. I tossed in bed with anxiety filling my mind. *Where is she?* I wondered. *Please, Lord, don't let anything happen to my child.*

Again, my daughter did not come home. As usual, I despaired and prepared for the worst. She might disappear for the night or for a week. There was no way to know. How can a mother's heart stand the uncertainty?

Now, I toss to my left side, I spot a glint of sunshine peeking underneath the blinds. The sun is coming up. A new day dawns. Then I hear a whisper in my heart: *"Be still, and know that I am God"* (Psalm 46:10). Hope is not gone. My hope rests in my God. I will not despair when the silence of the night screams fear into my head.

My daughter might not have come through the front door last night, but God slipped through the window this morning to give me hope.

Why are you downcast, O my soul? Why so disturbed within me? Put your hope in God, for I will yet praise him, my

Savior.... By day the LORD directs his love, at night his song is with me— a prayer to the God of my life.
—Psalm 42:5, 8

*F*ather, _____ did not come home again. My soul is downcast. I am disturbed. Help me not to despair over my wild child, _____. Help me to put my hope in You. I ask You to help _____ learn to place hope in You as personal Savior. By day, direct Your love to _____ and by night allow Your song to be our prayers to You. In Jesus's name. Amen.

———— ◆ ◆ ◆ ————

Elevator of Emotions

M y child held so much potential. He excelled in school with a grade point average far above his classmates. Athleticism oozed from his muscular body. Musically, he was spoken of as a child prodigy. My mother's heart held those dreams for my child.

But somewhere, somehow, he strayed off the track of success. My child started smoking cigarettes and graduated to inhaling marijuana fumes. His surpassing academics slid first to lethargy, then to failure. Apathy replaced athletics. Musical interest migrated to indifference. He went from the top to the bottom of life.

My child's decline into the basement of my hopes grips my heart with dread. My own obsessive ride from pride to disbelief and from disbelief into depression feels like a free fall off a cliff. *When will my child stop going downhill? Where will the elevator of my emotional upheaval land?*

Yet I recall the potential of my child's life. I feel hope begin to rise up in me. My faith surges upwards as I recall, *"'For I know the plans I have for you,' says the LORD. 'They are plans for good and not for disaster, to give you a future and a hope'"* (Jeremiah 29:11, NLT). The

14

depression begins to lift and I press on toward God. My hope for my child lies at the top with Him.

And hope does not disappoint us, because God has poured out his love into our hearts by the Holy Spirit, whom he has given us.
—Romans 5:5

*F*ather, hope will not disappoint _____ and me because You have poured out Your love into our hearts by the Holy Spirit. Give _____ the Holy Spirit, whom You have a desire to give to each of us. I wait in hope and expectation of Your work in _____'s life. In Jesus's name. Amen.

◆ ◆ ◆

Weak Knees

My knees shake. I have no idea what my child is doing in her rebellion. The silent phone stares back at me. My rattled nerves wait for it to jangle. At the same time, I dread to pick up the receiver to hear bad news. What is that saying: "No news is good news"?

I lay my Bible across the chair. I kneel before it and randomly open it. My eyes fall on a highlighted verse: *"Be strong and take heart, all you who hope in the Lord"* (Psalm 31:24). Oh, God is so good. I do hope in the Lord! I know He is able to take care of any situations that arise with my child. However, my mother's heart needs reminding that, when my knees tremble and my thoughts run amuck with fear, my God will come to me.

Yesterday, my child disappeared into rebellion. Today, my child hides her activities from me. Tomorrow, the phone may ring with bad news. Nevertheless, my God is the same every day. *"Jesus Christ is the same yesterday and today and forever"* (Hebrews 13:8). I will stay on weak knees and continue to pray for my wayward child, for I know my God will come to this state of affairs.

Strengthen the feeble hands, steady the knees that give way; say to those with fearful hearts, "Be strong, do not fear; your God will come."
—Isaiah 35:3–4

*D*ear Lord, steady my feeble knees as I pray for _____. Although my heart fears for _____, my hope is in You. Bring _____ to the point of saying, "My God has come, even in my rebellion." In Jesus's name. Amen.

———————— ◆ ◆ ◆ ————————

Perilous Exploits

Invincible. Indestructible. Insane. My son lives on the edge of danger. He calls it "living in the extreme." I call it foolish and reckless. My son's life dangles by a thin thread from the perilous exploits. As far as he is concerned, life is worthwhile only on a dare.

Daredevil. Determined. Depressed. His grim face searches for the next thrill. It frightens me because of what I see behind the resolved eyes. Eyes shadowed by an unspoken unhappiness. A deep darkness appears to seek a suicidal end. He adds more danger to each extreme thrill—drugs and drag racing, whiskey and white water rapids, pot and parachuting, and methamphetamine and mountain climbing. My son reeks of substance abuse and unhappiness.

Unhappy. Unstable. Unfulfilled. For years, my son's inner turmoil has prodded him to search for an escape. Adventures into sex, alcohol, and drugs leave him lacking a life of satisfaction. Extreme sports lure him with the potential to leave it all behind with an exhilarating end and no excuses.

Excuses. Excess. Exhaustion. I sense his frantic thoughts as he hunts the next reckless feat. Yet all my son needs to experience is the indescribable, immortal, and ineffable Lord God. Only in Christ will my son find fulfillment, contentment, and meaning to erratic life.

He has delivered us from such a deadly peril, and he will deliver us. On him we have set our hope that he will continue to deliver us, as you help us by your prayers. Then many will give thanks on our behalf for the gracious favor granted us in answer to the prayers of many.
—2 Corinthians 1:10–11

*D*ear Lord, deliver _____ from these deadly perils. On You we have set our hope that You will continue to deliver _____, as You help us, including by Your prayers. Then many will give thanks on behalf of _____ for the gracious favor granted in answer to my prayers. In Jesus's name. Amen.

———————— ◆ ◆ ◆ ————————

Apron Strings

*C*hildren! Sometimes when I am troubled, I cannot remember why I wanted any!

My mother says, "God allows children to grow into teenagers so that you can let them go easier. What if they were to remain as darling as they were as toddlers? It would break our hearts when they left home. But don't give up hope; you'll both eventually like each other again."

It is hard to believe that we will ever again have a loving parent-child relationship. Dislike for each other creates disharmony throughout the day. We pass each other without looking in the other's eyes. I say, "Excuse me," if we accidentally bump in the hallway. However, my motherly love longs for reconciliation.

"Patient in affliction." Yes, that certainly applies to parents of wild children. I wait in attempted patience while my child unknowingly afflicts pain to my heart. I relate to Proverbs 10:1: *"A wise son brings joy to his father, but a foolish son grief to his mother."* I grieve over my child's foolishness that overrules the godly wisdom taught in our home.

My child wants to cut the apron strings from our parent-child relationship. I must learn not to allow each snip of the string to sting my heart. But, oh, I do pray that my child would learn to mature in wisdom, instead of foolishness.

> *Be joyful in hope, patient in affliction, faithful in prayer.*
> —Romans 12:12

*O*h, Lord Jesus, teach me to be joyful in hope for the right outcome for _____. Although _____ causes me affliction, train me to be patient. Encourage me to continue to be faithful in prayer for _____. In Your name, I pray. Amen.

◆ ◆ ◆

Vaporized Dreams

*L*ike a mist, my child's dreams vaporized. Each time he tried to walk through an open door to pursue his passion, the door swung shut. His frustration resulted in anger at God. My child gave up on prayer and waiting for God's timing. With dispirited weariness, my son turned from the Lord to artificial hopes. Now he numbs his disappointment with sex, alcohol, and whatever else will silence the emotional pain.

As his parent, I witness the truth of God's Word: *"Where there is no vision, the people perish"* (Proverbs 29:18, KJV). My child is perishing within his vaporized dreams.

In panic, I attempt to encourage my child to still seek his goals in life. My maternal instinct searches out possibilities and probabilities. However, my manipulation stalls as I try to pull strings for my son's vision to become more than a fading mirage. With resignation, I realize I cannot fix the problem.

My God will renew my son's dreams when the time is right, but in the meantime, I need to be an example to my son. I will wait on the Lord in hope.

Even youths grow tired and weary, and young men stumble and fall; but those who hope in the Lord will renew their strength. They will soar on wings like eagles; they will run and not grow weary, they will walk and not be faint.
—Isaiah 40:30–31

*O*h Father, _____ has grown tired and weary. _____ has stumbled and fallen. Restore _____'s hope in You, and renew the strength of his dreams for life. Teach _____ to soar on wings like eagles. Help _____ to run and to not grow weary. Show _____ how to walk and not depend on artificial hope. In Jesus's name. Amen.

◆ ◆ ◆

Stuffed

Stuff. It spills from closets and drawers. It clutters the carpet of the bedroom. My daughter's obsession with stuff influences her every thought. She spends every dime she makes on the next purchase. She reaches for the shiny plastic credit card when the money is gone.

Credit collectors call her new cell phone every day. My daughter ignores those she considers her harassers. Then she hunts for the next eager lender to supply money for her must-have mania habit. The fear

19

of financial ruin and bankruptcy do not deter the next buying binge.

What fissure in my daughter's heart is she attempting to fill? Why does she place hope in material possessions for her happiness?

Whatever the reasons, she will not find contentment in the material wealth of junk The strappy red sandals, the newest media player, and the prettiest pair of dangly chandelier earrings only prove to be a temporary fix for her needy feelings. The pricey pair of worn and torn jeans only displays to me the hole in her heart.

I understand that she needs to place her hope in Christ. She does not. So all I can do is pray for her. I pray that *stuff* will lose its hypnotic influence over her. That soon she will understand she needs to place her expectation in God, who alone provides contentment and fulfillment.

Command those who are rich in this present world not to be arrogant nor to put their hope in wealth, which is so uncertain, but to put their hope in God, who richly provides us with everything for our enjoyment.
—1 Timothy 6:17

*L*ord Jesus, somehow help _____ not to be arrogant, nor to put hope in wealth. Wealth is so uncertain. Help _____ to place hope in You, who so richly provides us with everything for our enjoyment. In Your name, I pray. Amen.

——————— ◆ ◆ ◆ ———————

Incorrigible

*P*eople say, "Give up! Why waste your time on him? He is hopeless." I refuse to give up hope for my son. Yes, by human measures he may seem to be without hope, but not in the sight of the Lord God Almighty. *"Is anything too hard for the LORD?"* (Genesis 18:14).

People say, "He will never change."

My son's rebellion rages against authority. My son's illegal actions have landed him in prison many times. The court system describes him as "incorrigible." I refuse the notion that my child cannot change. I recall, *"The LORD sets prisoners free"* (Psalm 146:7).

They say, "He's been irredeemable for years. No one can save him."

My son's wanton ways have wreaked havoc in every aspect of his life. He does not care about anyone.

I rebuff the naysayers' thoughts that the Lord cannot save my child. God cares about my son. *"Rise up and help us; redeem us because of your unfailing love"* (Psalm 44:26).

I refuse to give up hope for my son.

And when he prayed, the LORD listened to him and was moved by his request for help. So the LORD let Manasseh return to Jerusalem and to his kingdom. Manasseh had finally realized that the LORD alone is God!...

Manasseh's prayer, the account of the way God answered him, and an account of all his sins and unfaithfulness are recorded in The Record of the Seers.
—2 Chronicles 33:13, 19 (NLT)

*L*ord God Almighty, I ask that _____ will turn to You in desperation and pray for help. Listen to _____ and be moved by _____'s request. Allow _____ to return to the faith and home. Somehow, finally make _____ realize that You alone are God! In Jesus's name. Amen.

———————— ◆ ◆ ◆ ————————

"But God..."

*"B*ut God"—these two words completely fulfill any hope, expectation, or dream I hold for my wild child. I cling to God's Word to help me through this time, as my child becomes a wayfarer from the faith. Throughout Scripture, the phrase *"But God"* repeats the expectation of God's power to the reader.

Therefore, when despair overrides all other emotions, I recite, *"But God."* What I am not for my wild child, He is. What I cannot do for my child, He can. My only hope is in the faithfulness of God to reconcile my child to Him and to me.

At times, I tremble in fear of the unknowable future of my child. I quake, but God remains steady. I relate to the psalmist who wrote, *"My flesh and my heart may fail, **but God** is the strength of my heart and my portion forever"* (Psalm 73:26; bold is author's emphasis). God is my strength and my portion forever. He will be for my wild child too.

So I hope in God. My knees bow in prayer instead of knock with fear because of two words: *But God.*

But God does not take away life; instead, he devises ways so that a banished person may not remain estranged from him.
—2 Samuel 14:14

*D*ear God, You do not take away life. I know You will devise ways so that my banished wild child, _____, will no longer be estranged from You. You will accept _____ into Your family. I pray this in Jesus's name. Amen.

◆ ◆ ◆

Whispers of Hope to My Wild Child

Dear Wild Child,

My child, did you know that the word *hope* translates accurately to "expectation" in many biblical contexts? That thrills me! Yes, I will always carry hope in my heart for the promise of abundant life in your future; more importantly, I wait in expectation. I believe deep within my soul you will come into the knowledge of salvation through the Lord Jesus Christ.

However, I must wait quietly. I know you have been frustrated by my preaching at you. Those words have resulted in pushing you further away from the Lord and me. My new mantra is this: *"Don't talk too much, for it fosters sin. Be sensible and turn off the flow!"* (Proverbs 10:19 NLT). I am going to turn off my flow of words.

Instead of me rattling on about my dreams for your life, I want to hear about *your* hopes and expectations of the future. Will you grant me a peek? I promise to listen without adding my own commentary.

So until then, dear child, I will hope, with great expectation, to hear from you. Until then, I will wait quietly.

The Lord is good to those whose hope is in him, to the one who seeks him; it is good to wait quietly for the salvation of the Lord.
—Lamentations 3:25–26

 *D*ear Lord, be good to _____ as I wait in hope for _____ to learn to seek You. Teach me to wait quietly for Your salvation to come to _____. I will wait quietly in expectation. In Your name, I pray. Amen.

◆ ◆ ◆

2

Whispers of Forgiveness

High-Efficiency Wash

The new front-load washing machine whirls the dirty clothes. The sales representative tells us that because it does not have an agitator, it is not as hard on the clothing. It uses less water and less electricity. Plus, the clothing will be spotless.

Hmmm. I wish I could put my child in the new high-efficiency machine. My child's life is agitated and dirty. He tumbles around in sin, allowing it to cling to his soul. Then he wears it proudly for the world to see.

My child, on occasion, will pretend to be clean, usually when he wants something from someone who disapproves of mucky stains in his life. He whitewashes the outside to masquerade a false morality.

However, no matter how much my child tries to pretend, he still appears to be murky gray. No amount of chlorine bleach can erase his heart of sin. Yet I know that God can clean up the worst of sinners, because I have been there myself.

With my child in my thoughts, I purchase the expensive washing machine; at least my clothing will be spotless. And with a prayer on my lips, I ask God to fulfill His own high-efficiency cleansing in my child's life. I yearn for my child to be a walking, talking testimony for

God's cleansing power. I know someday he will desire to be clean, and he will pray, *"Soak me in your laundry and I'll come out clean, scrub me and I'll have a snow-white life"* (Psalm 51:7 *The Message*).

> *"'I will cleanse them from all the sin they have committed against me and will forgive all their sins of rebellion against me.'"*
> —Jeremiah 33:8

*L*ord God, cleanse _____ from all the sin that he/she has committed against You. Forgive _____ for all the sins of rebellion that have been committed against You. In Jesus's name. Amen.

———————— ◆ ◆ ◆ ————————

Denial

The shame-filled regret shadows my child's face. My child cannot seem to move past the repetitive reviling thoughts of past behaviors. Satan whispers, *You can't go back now; look at what you've done. God will never forgive you, because by your actions and words, you've denied Him.*

My child feels the unpardonable sin has been committed. He does not turn back to God, because he believes it is too late to walk in faith. He failed. He has given up. Again, these are lies of the accuser.

I know because I have walked in the same shame-filled shoes. For years, I felt I could not call myself a Christian because of my years of rebellion. But oh, how mistaken I was! God pursued. God wooed. Christ forgave. Christ commissioned.

Although I attempt to persuade my child of God's love and forgiveness, my child cannot fathom this. The truth of God's forgiveness must come from the very heart of God to the broken heart of my child. Jesus will appear as the risen Savior to my child. Hallelujah!

But Peter said, "Man, I don't know what you are talking about." And as soon as he said these words, the rooster crowed. At that moment the Lord turned and looked at Peter. Then Peter remembered that the Lord had said, "Before the rooster crows tomorrow morning, you will deny me three times." And Peter left the courtyard, crying bitterly.
—Luke 22:60–62 (NLT)

"The Lord has really risen! He appeared to Peter!"
—Luke 24:34 (NLT)

$\mathcal{L}$ord Jesus, You knew before it happened that _____ would deny You by actions and words. _____ has wept bitter tears over the mistakes, but feels worthless and unforgiven. Lord Jesus, woo _____ back to You. Show Your forgiveness to _____, just as You did when I denied You. In Your name, I pray. Amen.

◆ ◆ ◆

The Sneak

Her brown eyes fill with tears of false indignation. My daughter swears that she has not been out carousing. Her voice trembles as she says, "Mom, you never believe me. Why don't you trust me?"

I waiver for a moment. *Maybe she is telling the truth this time.* My mother's heart wants to believe her words. And I could just end the upcoming battle before it starts. No tantrums. It would be so much easier if I just said, "OK."

However, I know deep within that she is lying to my face. My mother's intuition warns me. We have been down this road so many times before. I must acknowledge the fact that my daughter is a sneak and a liar. I will not back down and give in simply to keep the peace.

27

I hear the sound of my own mother's voice coming out of my mouth, "I wasn't born yesterday. I know where you've been."

The battle begins. The tantrum I dread begins to roll out of my sneaky daughter. The war will probably wage on until dark. I will go to bed exhausted, but I will not be defeated by the cunning deception of my child.

I recall my own youth. I was a sneak too. And thankfully, my mother "wasn't born yesterday" either.

Once we, too, were foolish and disobedient. We were misled by others and became slaves to many wicked desires and evil pleasures.... But then God our Savior showed us his kindness and love. He saved us, not because of the good things we did, but because of his mercy. He washed away our sins and gave us a new life through the Holy Spirit.
—Titus 3:3–5 (NLT)

*F*ather, I was foolish and disobedient, just like _____. I know _____ is a slave to many wicked desires and evil pleasures.... But God, show _____ Your love and kindness. Save _____. Wash away the sins of _____ and give her/him a new life through the Holy Spirit. In Jesus's name. Amen.

◆ ◆ ◆

Paralyzed

People inform my daughter that she has committed the ultimate sin. Scared and confused, she ignorantly went to a medical clinic to end a surprise pregnancy. Hurtful words haunt my daughter. She masks the taunts with whiskey and other drugs. Still, through the fog of drunkenness, she hears the repeated accusation, "Murderer!"

Physical, emotional, and spiritual pain resulted from the decision to end her pregnancy. Her body has recovered from the physical pain. Drugs and alcohol numb the emotional pain. However, she lies paralyzed in her sin. Until she turns to Jesus and accepts His forgiveness, she will not experience spiritual healing, but she needs help getting to Him.

She needs the Christian community to respond with care, not react in repulsion. My daughter needs someone to reach out to her in love and mercy. No more condemnation. She needs a loving friend to bring her to the feet of Jesus. No more hateful words. She needs a mentor, perhaps someone who has walked in the same pain, to carry her showers of tears and thunderstorms of heartache underneath the umbrella of divine grace. No more judgment.

So, as only a mother can do, I wait and I pray for someone who cares enough about my spiritually paralyzed daughter to lower her into the lap of Jesus.

Four men arrived carrying a paralyzed man on a mat. They couldn't get to Jesus through the crowd, so they dug through the clay roof above his head. Then they lowered the sick man on his mat, right down in front of Jesus. Seeing their faith, Jesus said to the paralyzed man, "My son, your sins are forgiven."
—Mark 2:3–5 (NLT)

*O*h Lord Jesus, please touch someone's heart with compassion to bring _____ right down in front of You. Allow _____ to see their faithfulness and to accept forgiveness when You say, "_____, your sins are forgiven." I pray this in Your name. Amen.

———————— ◆ ◆ ◆ ————————

Deviled Eggs

As a little girl, she adored deviled eggs. In fact, it was the only type of eggs she would eat. The spices whipped into the yolk hid the eggs' primary taste.

Sadly, deviled eggs are a metaphor for my daughter's life now. It is spiced up with peccadillo, and she cannot taste the bitterness of the sin.

"I am just having fun, Mom. I am not hurting anyone. I am not doing anything illegal; everybody does it. You're just old-fashioned," she declares with a saucy attitude.

However, what she does not realize is that I have danced on the same tables. I have drunk the booze that enabled me to lose my inhibitions. I know the reality of Titus 3:3: *"At one time we too were foolish, disobedient, deceived and enslaved by all kinds of passions and pleasures."* The pleasurable spice of sin will enslave anyone who chases after it.

I share with my beloved daughter the metaphor of the deviled eggs. She laughs.

Ashamed and embarrassed, I confess to her my own history with enjoyable sin.

She looks down uncomfortably. Then she laughs, "Oh Mom, you're a deviled egg. Like you ever did anything like that!"

If we claim to be without sin, we deceive ourselves and the truth is not in us. If we confess our sins, he is faithful and just and will forgive us our sins and purify us from all unrighteousness.
—1 John 1:8–9

Father, allow _____ to acknowledge his/her sinful life. Do not allow _____ to deceive himself/herself. I ask that _____ will confess his/her sins. I know You are faithful and just and will forgive _____'s sins and purify him/her from all unrighteousness. In Jesus's name. Amen.

◆ ◆ ◆

Bad Blood

The nurse poked and prodded to find a vein in my son's arm. He grimaced as the needle went deeper into the muscled arm. Finally, a flow of blood began to fill the tube and drain into the glass vial. My son's face paled, and he turned his eyes toward the medical chart hanging on the wall.

Grateful for this begrudged blood donation, I patted his knee in approval and encouragement. Something between a growl and grunt came from between his clenched teeth. I translated it as, "Don't ever ask me to do this again for him."

His critically ill father was in desperate need of a blood donation. Fortunately, my son shares the same blood type. Unfortunately, it is the only thing they hold in common.

My son despises his father. He resents the harsh treatment he received as a child from the old-school military dad. Unforgiveness courses through his soul. The old saying, "Bad blood lies between them," applies to their relationship. Father and son need to forgive each other. They need to let Jesus's blood flow into the veins of their souls, producing grace and understanding for each other.

I begged my son to donate. He agreed reluctantly, yet it is a step in the right direction toward forgiving his dad. This donation may be the one that replaces bad blood with a transfusion of good blood, both physically and spiritually.

In him we have redemption through his blood, the forgiveness of sins, in accordance with the riches of God's grace that he

lavished on us with all wisdom and understanding.
—Ephesians 1:7–8

*L*ord Jesus, may _____ have redemption through Your blood. Help _____ to ask You for the forgiveness of his/her sin of hatred. Then in accordance with the riches of Your grace, lavish on _____ wisdom and understanding of past hurts in his/her life. In Your name, I pray. Amen.

──────── ◆ ◆ ◆ ────────

Lord, Again?

I am tired of forgiving my daughter. My antagonism toward her borders between intense dislike and complete indifference. Today I do not care where she goes or what she does. I feel both aggression and apathy.

The lack of concern frightens me. *Has she shoved me so far away emotionally that I don't even want to be bothered by asking God to help me forgive her again? Have I reached the point of no return with my child?* These disturbing questions float through my hurt and angry feelings. Suddenly a different thought filters through: *"If you forgive those who sin against you, your heavenly Father will forgive you"* (Matthew 6:14 NLT).

Arghhh! One of the hazards of being a Christian mother is the Holy Spirit nudges me to do what a follower of Christ does—namely, forgive. I think of Elizabeth Barrett Browning's verse, "How do I love thee? Let me count the ways." I could pen a similar line for my daughter, "How do I forgive you? Let me count the ways." Oh yeah, *"Love never gives up. Love cares more for others than for self.... [Love] doesn't keep score of the sins of others"* (1 Corinthians 13:4–5 *The Message*).

OK! All right! I forgive her, Lord. Again.

Then Peter came to Jesus and asked, "Lord, how many times shall I forgive my brother when he sins against me? Up to seven times?"

Jesus answered, "I tell you, not seven times, but seventy-seven times."

—Matthew 18:21–22

*L*ord Jesus, how many times must I forgive _____ when _____ sins against me? I feel as if I have already forgiven _____ seventy-seven times. I realize the point is to keep forgiving without keeping a record. Help me to forgive _____ once again. In Your name. Amen.

————————— ◆ ◆ ◆ —————————

Instant Recall

My ex-husband had a photographic memory. It amazed me that after he read a book, he could instantly and even a week later recall the pages' exact contents. It seemed like magic to me, but to him it was a normal, everyday occurrence—nothing special.

Unfortunately, my wild child did not inherit the memory gift. Every single time my son commits a transgression, he states, "I forgot." He gives me a blank stare that attempts to translate, "It's not my fault. I just forgot."

However, I know better. My child knows the rules. He has been taught right from wrong.

He commits the same acts of defiance repeatedly. If he forgets, it is because he chooses not to remember. He does not have amnesia, as he wants me to believe; he is outright rebellious.

Only God can change my son's heart. I yearn for him to come back into a relationship with Christ. I want my son to repent of his stubborn denial of his sins. I pray to hear him say, *"The Sovereign Lord has opened my ears, and I have not been rebellious; I have not drawn back"* (Isaiah 50:5).

I know the Lord God has instant recall of His mercy and love for my wild child. God does not forget.

Remember, O LORD, your great mercy and love,
for they are from of old.
Remember not the sins of my youth
and my rebellious ways;
according to your love remember me,
for you are good, O LORD.
—Psalm 25:6–7

*O*h Lord, remember Your great mercy and love for _____.
Remember not the sins of _____'s youth and _____'s
rebellious ways. According to Your love, remember _____,
for You are good, oh Lord. In Jesus's name. Amen.

———————— ◆ ◆ ◆ ————————

Vinegar and Soda

Chemistry was always a mystery to me. What I do know is the common experiment of vinegar and soda. If you mix the two ingredients, the acidic vinegar reacts with the baking soda. The mixture becomes unstable and erupts into froth. The two ingredients do not blend; instead, they have a chemical meltdown.

My relationship with my daughter mimics that experiment. She is the acidic personality, and I react with an emotional eruption. As hard as I try not to blow up at her razor-sharp remarks, I cannot contain myself. The steam of anger surges up, and before I know it, we are out of control with hurtful words being hurled at each other.

This morning, our argument produced wounds that could last

a lifetime. We both slammed the door on our mother-daughter relationship. She left in tears of anger; I wept with hurt feelings.

Finally, I decided to take some time alone with God. I picked up the devotional, *My Utmost for His Highest*, written by Oswald Chambers. I turned to the day of June 17th and read the words, "I have never met a person I could despair of or lose all hope for, after discerning what lies in me apart from God."

I felt God's Spirit comfort me. No, I cannot despair over my daughter's acidic words, because within me lies the same spiteful behavior. Only through the grace of Christ will we be able to find love and forgiveness for each other.

I think when she comes home, I will show her the vinegar and soda experiment. Then I will ask for her forgiveness and allow Jesus to work a little good chemistry between us.

Be kind and compassionate to one another, forgiving each other, just as in Christ God forgave you.
—Ephesians 4:32

$\mathcal{L}$ord Jesus, teach _____ and me to be kind and compassionate to each other. Help _____ to forgive me and me to forgive _____. Let us both learn to forgive as You forgave us. In Your name, I pray. Amen.

◆ ◆ ◆

Whispers of Forgiveness to My Wild Child

Dear Wild Child,

It is said parents should not live their lives through their children. I agree wholeheartedly, except for one dimension of the advice. A mother desires to experience joy and fulfillment in her child's life.

Your life is yours to live. It is your decision whether you want to be an astronaut, a thief, a ballet dancer, or a con artist. Some choices in life lend themselves to contentment and joy. Other decisions cause heartbreak and hardship. Of course, as your mom, I would like you to choose contentment and joy over heartbreak and hardship. But it is your choice.

It may seem as though I want you to do everything my way, but I do not. However, I do want you to experience the joy that comes from forgiveness of sins that the Lord Jesus graciously grants to anyone who asks.

On that note, I ask that you forgive me for anything that I have done to cause you pain and hurt. I am truly sorry. Please know I forgive you too. Let's allow it to be "ditto forgiveness." I feel joy already; I pray you do, too, my wild child.

Oh, what joy for those whose rebellion is forgiven, whose sin is put out of sight! Yes, what joy for those whose record the LORD has cleared of sin, whose lives are lived in complete honesty!
—Psalm 32:1–2 (NLT)

*H*eavenly Father, I desire for _____ to experience the joy when his/her rebellion is forgiven and is put out of sight. Yes, I want joy for _____ when You clear the record of his/her sin. Let _____ make the right choice and choose to live in complete honesty before You. In Jesus's name. Amen.

3

Whispers of Wisdom

Kindergarten of Maturity

Poor choices—my child excels at making them. She struts her independence and then does something so ridiculous that even she realizes she did not use good sense. It is amazing that she has such genius, but makes such unwise decisions.

My child refuses to acknowledge that the Sovereign God just might be able to help her with important life choices. Instead, she ridicules me for suggesting that reverence for God and prayer can lead her in the right direction. Proverbs 13:1 could have been written about my daughter: *"Intelligent children listen to their parents; foolish children do their own thing"* (*The Message*). She pulls away from God and me, like a five-year-old trying to cross a busy street by herself. Suddenly, she recognizes the danger and jumps back to the safety of the curb.

Although she looks like an adult, she is immature. I guess my child is in the kindergarten of maturity. Surely, someday she will realize that all wisdom comes from God. She will grow into her faith as she grows into womanhood.

In the meantime, I pray for wisdom from God to know how to help my child develop into a woman of godly wisdom.

Reverence for the LORD is the foundation of true wisdom.
The rewards of wisdom come to all who obey him.
Praise his name forever!
—Psalm 111:10 (NLT)

*D*ear Lord, instill in _____ reverence for You, the foundation of true wisdom. Teach _____ to understand the rewards of wisdom that come to all who obey You. Lord, show me how to respond to my child's poor choices. Then bring us to the point in the future where _____ and I will praise Your name forever. In Jesus's name. Amen.

◆ ◆ ◆

The Runaway

I was sitting at my desk working on household bills when I heard the gritty noise of her bedroom window slide open. Within seconds, a soft thud of two feet sounded as they hit the malleable dirt. Then the wooden blinds rattled as the wind blew through the open window.

My heart sank as I acknowledged to myself that my daughter had run away—again. *How many times am I going to have to go through this?* I wondered. *I do not even feel anger anymore—only a sense of total defeat. She perceives any act of my parenting as abuse and mistreatment. Every time she disagrees with me, she disappears for a few days.*

Although she usually stayed with friends, I trembled for her safety. I wanted to give up and let her do whatever she wanted. However, deep down, I knew that was not the answer to my daughter's insubordinate behavior.

In resignation, I picked up the phone to call my family and my pastor. Then, I began to call her friends. I could not call the police until she had been missing for at least 24 hours. Nevertheless, I did not waste that time; I prayed for the Lord to seek out my runaway and convince her to come home.

> *The angel of the Lord found Hagar beside a desert spring along the road to Shur. The angel said to her, "Hagar, Sarai's servant, where have you come from, and where are you going?"*
>
> *"I am running away from my mistress," she replied.*
>
> *Then the angel of the Lord said, "Return to your mistress and submit to her authority."*
>
> —Genesis 16:7–9 (NLT)

*L*ord God, You know where _____ is headed off to this time. Stop my child. Ask _____, "Where have you come from and where are you going?" Give _____ the wisdom to search his/her heart for the truth in our relationship. Encourage _____ to come home and submit to my authority as the mom. In Jesus's name. Amen.

◆ ◆ ◆

Bewitched

My son used to lead the church youth group. For years, my car sported a bumper sticker that read, "My child loves Jesus." For crying out loud, my son went on mission trips for 10 years. He performed all the correct churchy deeds.

Now who is this person who goes by my son's name? He is not the same Christian son that I touted to others. He is no longer the child that I pinned my Christian motherly pride upon. Now he is a kid like the ones I used to point to and smugly say, "My boy would never leave the faith like that one did! He loves the Lord."

"Pride goes before destruction, a haughty spirit before a fall" (Proverbs 16:18)—ah, a lesson harshly learned by this prideful mother. Because he did all the "right" things, I falsely assumed that he knew the Lord Jesus.

However, somewhere between religion and philosophy, my son became bewitched by false teaching. Bewitched by humanism. He no longer felt the need for a crucified Savior. He preferred to do life on his own merit.

"Mom, there is no absolute truth! You can believe those myths, but I am just going to be a good human being." Oh Lord, teach my son wisdom and truth.

You foolish Galatians! Who has bewitched you? Before your very eyes Jesus Christ was clearly portrayed as crucified. I would like to learn just one thing from you: Did you receive the Spirit by observing the law, or by believing what you heard? Are you so foolish? After beginning with the Spirit, are you now trying to attain your goal by human effort?
—Galatians 3:1–3

*O*h Father, I ask that You teach _____ the truth of Jesus Christ, the crucified Savior. Remove the foolish teaching from _____'s mind. Reveal to my child, _____, that good deeds cannot reap the goal of eternal life with You. In Jesus's name, Amen.

———————— ◆ ◆ ◆ ————————

Ids and Egos

"*I* can't help it. It's human nature to pursue pleasure. I am just following what my counselor has instructed me to do—to break free from the inhibitions that were produced in me by religion. And honestly, Mom, I am so happy."

Freud's theories resound in my child's head. *Ids, egos,* and *superegos* dictate that anything goes as long as it feels good and satisfies a personal desire. The pursuit of sensual pleasure influences every activity in my child's world. Id plus ego plus superego equal complete self-absorption.

To my child, biblical precepts are restrictive and antiquated. He refuses to acknowledge the truth of God's Word. But the Scriptures speak true wisdom. The author of Hebrews acknowledges that sensual self-indulgence is fun for a short time, giving the example of Moses and what his superego chose to do: *"Choosing rather to suffer affliction with the people of God, than to enjoy the pleasures of sin for a season"* (Hebrews 11:25 KJV). Look at what Moses got for refusing his id's desires; he became a friend of God.

A friend of God—yes, that is what my child needs to become. He needs to learn to listen to the Spirit instead of the wisdom of this world. His id needs to be squashed by the power of God's Spirit.

My message and my preaching were not with wise and persuasive words, but with a demonstration of the Spirit's power, so that your faith might not rest on men's wisdom, but on God's power.
—1 Corinthians 2:4–5

*O*h Lord Jesus, allow Your message to _____ to sound like wise and persuasive words. Let the demonstration of the Spirit's power influence _____ so that his faith might rest not on men's wisdom, but on Your power. In Jesus's name. Amen.

Obedience School

My dog used to disobey any house rule. Speckles would speckle the floor. He would run into the street. His nonstop barking annoyed the neighbors. All this continued until I made the decision to take my dog to obedience training. At doggy school, they taught me how to transform Speckles from an aggravating dog into a well-behaved canine companion. I wish it were that easy to mold my son from insubordination to compliance with the household rules.

Proverbs 13:24 states, *"If you refuse to discipline your children, it proves you don't love them; if you love your children, you will be prompt to discipline them"* (NLT). I love my son. Therefore, I attempted the "tough love" approach. It backfired. The tougher I became, the more rebellious he reacted. I threatened him with a military school. In retaliation, he bought military camouflage and disappeared into the foothills for four days until the local police finally "captured" him.

The difference between my dog and my son is that Speckles desires to please me. He begs for my praise. In contrast, my son purposely pushes my hot buttons, so I respond in frustration and accusation.

I am tired of other parents' suggestions and criticisms. No new disciplinary measures pop into my head. Exhaustion wears at me as I try to tether my son away from rebellious and reckless behaviors.

I need wisdom from God. I need it today!

If any of you lacks wisdom, he should ask God, who gives generously to all without finding fault, and it will be given to him.
—James 1:5

Father, I lack wisdom on how to discipline _____. I am asking for wisdom from You, knowing You give generously to all who ask. I know You will not find fault with my parenting skills, but will aid me in understanding how to discipline _____, whom

I love with all my heart. Help me to be prompt to discipline without succumbing to exhaustion. In Jesus's name. Amen.

◆ ◆ ◆

Long-Term Healthcare

I belong to the "sandwich generation." My parents need my care and my child needs help. I am being eaten alive between two needy generations. They each expect, require, and dictate my time, energy, and money. Both ends of this continuum—the silver-haired and the spiked, purple-haired—act out their emotions in orneriness. Their stubborn refusals to cooperate with me make me want to pull *my* hair out.

My parents need to reside in a long-term health care facility. "No, we won't go. You can help us. We took care of you for years." Oh no.

My child refuses to get an education or a job. "I don't want to. You can't make me. I don't need your advice." Yikes!

I examine my limited options. I need wisdom to deal with this type of bologna. I seek my Lord. I ask for wisdom.

I discover my parents have a long-term healthcare policy. It will pay a part-time medical assistant to help with their care. I find a community service that offers free taxi service for my parents' appointments. Hallelujah!

Now, I must attend to my child's needs. I pray for understanding. I pray that the bottom of my generational sandwich will begin to mature, begin to understand that the Holy One provides long-term healthcare of every type.

With optimism, I head for the kitchen. I grab the grape jelly (which matches my child's dyed hair color) and proceed to make a peanut butter and jelly sandwich—my child's favorite. Maybe its sweetness will overcome the orneriness.

"The fear of the LORD is the beginning of wisdom,
and knowledge of the Holy One is understanding.
For through me your days will be many, and years will be
added to your life."
—Proverbs 9:10–11

*H*oly One, teach _____ to fear You. I ask that
_____ come to the knowledge and understanding of You.
In addition, Lord, add years to _____'s life. In Jesus's
name. Amen.

◆ ◆ ◆

Hoodwinked Hoodlum

My wild child supposes he is getting away with the things he is doing behind my back. (Does he not know mothers have eyes in the back of their heads?) He acts so innocently Christian, then springs into hoodlum mode and traipses off with his hooligan friends. It is like living with a Dr. Jekyll and Mr. Hyde, a saint and sinner.

I am not unaware of my wild child's indulgence in the world of sin. Neither is God deceived. It is my hooligan who is hoodwinked by thinking he is getting away with all of his behaviors.

My son is of age. I cannot stop him from sowing seeds of sin that will grow into bushels of trouble. God cannot be mocked. God has a word for people who believe as my wild child does: *"They sow the wind and reap the whirlwind"* (Hosea 8:7).

So I wait. I wait for the hood to be yanked off the deceived eyes of my son. He will eventually discover that although he surmised he was conning everyone, including God, it was he who had been mislead.

Then my hoodwinked child will discover a whirlwind that will twirl him into sowing for the Spirit of God and eternal life.

Until then, I watch with eyes in the back of my head and pray.

Do not be deceived: God cannot be mocked. A man reaps what he sows. The one who sows to please his sinful nature, from that nature will reap destruction; the one who sows to please the Spirit, from the Spirit will reap eternal life.
—Galatians 6:7–8

*S*weet Jesus, do not allow _____ to be deceived. Let _____ understand that God cannot be mocked. _____ will reap what he/she sows. Right now, _____ sows to please the sinful nature, but from that nature _____ will reap destruction. I ask for _____ to learn to please You and to reap eternal life. In Your name. Amen.

———————— ◆ ◆ ◆ ————————

Wise Old Owl

My bookworm wiggles his way through mounds of textbooks. He reads and digests every intellectually profound thing he can put his hands on. My son graduated from the top universities. Titles and letters follow his name, making him sound important.

My bookworm went away to college. He gained an education, but lost his faith. He claims that the Bible is historical fiction. "What can I learn from it? It's just a mythology," he says smugly.

Ah, but look at his life. He jumps from financial fiascos to lurid love affairs to career catastrophes. Where is the intelligence in his everyday life? My bookworm lacks street smarts. Or as grandma would say, "That child has no horse sense! He's a dumb donkey pretending to be a wise old owl."

Yes, my child is not as smart as he pretends. He needs to discover the truth of God's Word and follow the advice of Proverbs 1:

> *Let the wise listen and add to their learning, and let the discerning get guidance—for understanding proverbs and parables, the sayings and riddles of the wise.*
> —Proverbs 1:5–6

Studious bookworm, dumb donkey, pretend wise old owl—that's my child. Thankfully, I believe in a God who is wise and powerful enough to draw in my child to recognize the truth of Scripture, eventually.

Until then, I am wise enough to pray the power of God's Word over him every day.

> *All Scripture is God-breathed and is useful for teaching, rebuking, correcting and training in righteousness, so that the man of God may be thoroughly equipped for every good work.*
> —2 Timothy 3:16–17

*L*ord Jesus, get through to _____ that all Scripture is God-breathed and is useful for teaching, rebuking, correcting, and training in righteousness. Give _____ the knowledge of the truth of Your Word so he/she may be a child of God thoroughly equipped for every good work. In Your name. Amen.

——————— ◆ ◆ ◆ ———————

Bits and Pieces

The pain I feel over my child's situation is almost unbearable. As a horrified bystander views an auto accident unfold, I watch with trepidation as God deals with my wild child's rebellion. I am wise enough to know that it is for her good, but still my heart screams, "No! God, no!"

For years I have prayed, "Lord, please bring her back to You." Now I see His hand unfolding in her life. Results of her reckless behavior are slowly beginning to return her to God. Words from Old Testament prophecy play out before me:

> *"Because you rage against me and because your insolence has reached my ears, I will put my hook in your nose and my bit in your mouth, and I will make you return by the way you came."*
> —Isaiah 37:29

God has placed a bit of consequence in her life to return her back to Himself. She will return to the faith, but only through painful circumstances. I watch in silent prayer.

It hurts my wild child. It pains my mother's heart. However, the result will be well worth the agony when my child finally acknowledges that life with the Lord God is precious and worth every bit of pain she suffers for her past rebellion.

> *It was good for me to be afflicted so that I might learn your decrees. The law from your mouth is more precious to me than thousands of pieces of silver and gold.*
> —Psalm 119:71–72

*L*ord God, it is good for _____ to be afflicted, so that _____ might learn Your decrees. Make the law from Your mouth more precious to _____ than thousands of pieces of silver and gold. In Jesus's name. Amen.

◆ ◆ ◆

Whispers of Wisdom to My Wild Child

Dear Wild Child,

I think the sweetest taste created by nature is honey. Can you believe

47

this golden, syrupy delicacy is created by itty-bitty bees buzzing in and out of flowers? Our Creator is quite imaginative!

When you were a baby, I used to dip a pacifier in honey to coax you to take it. You would not. (Now the wisdom of pediatricians tells moms not to give an infant honey. How times change!)

My precious child, some wisdom changes, but God's wisdom endures forever. I would ask you to find this type of wisdom in your life. Bees produce honey; the Bible provides a sweet wisdom to the person who studies it. *"How sweet are your words to my taste; they are sweeter than honey. Your commandments give me understanding; no wonder I hate every false way of life"* (Psalm 119:103–104 NLT).

I used to offer you a pacifier, an artificial soother, dipped in sugar to make it tasty, but now I offer you a real source of comfort that is sweet and meaty in and of itself: the Word of God. You would not accept the calming influence of the pacifier as a baby. Will you now receive this offering of real comfort: a new Bible, brimming with God's sweet and nourishing wisdom that will produce an eternal hope for your future?

Know also that wisdom is sweet to your soul; if you find it, there is a future hope for you, and your hope will not be cut off.
—Proverbs 24:14

*L*ord Jesus, reveal to _____ that Your wisdom is sweet to the soul. Give _____ the knowledge that if he/she finds wisdom, there will be a future hope and _____ will not be cut off. In Your name. Amen.

◆ ◆ ◆

4

Whispers of Relationships

Fresh Start

My family needs a fresh start. The emotional baggage we haul around exhausts us emotionally and physically. What we need is a spanking-new type of family fondness. Well, maybe not *spanking* new because right now that is the wrong thing to have on my mind—spanking the blazes out of my child.

She is too old to be punished and yet too young to not be corrected. I could put her on restriction, but that only makes me and everyone else in our home miserable. I prefer not to have to watch her sulk. Her perpetual pouts and incessant whining grate on my nerves. Here is the truth: I do not like her *behavior*, but I do love *her*.

I want to be a godly mom. I need to be the one to show the love of Jesus, as He displays His love for me when I am being strong willed and difficult. So I will plead for a fresh start in these family relationships. I will choose to like her, even when I would like to spank her behaviors away.

Now we look inside, and what we see is that anyone united with the Messiah gets a fresh start, is created new.... All this comes from the God who settled the relationship between us

49

and him, and then called us to settle our relationships with each other.
—2 Corinthians 5:17–18 (*The Message*)

*D*ear Jesus, allow me to look inside and see that anyone united with You gets a fresh start and is created new. I ask You to settle the relationship between You and _____. Please assist me in settling the relationship between _____ and myself. In Your name. Amen.

◆ ◆ ◆

Holy Tattoo

*S*kulls grin at me from across the room. As my son's arm reaches for his water, a snake's blood-red eye winks at me. I recall hanging my son's crayon pictures on the fridge. Pastel Sunday School portraits of the Jesus he loved. Now he displays colorful artwork of a different genre—on his own skin.

Sullen indifference replaces the sweet excitement my little boy used to possess. I wonder where the young artist-child hides inside this young man I hardly recognize. Surely, he resides in my son's soul still.

Smiling at the memories, I ask, "Son, can I get you a refill? I'm headed to the kitchen."

Without looking up, he nods.

I stop at the fridge to fill up the glass and whisper to God, "Bring back the boy of the crayon days. Help him to feel the excitement again! Let him remember how he colorfully displayed Your love for him each week. Lord, tattoo his heart with Your love. Give my son a tattoo of holiness. Fill him with Your love, just as I fill up this glass."

As I hand the brimming glass to my son, I know God heard my prayer. I smile down at my son's colorful arm, but this time, I wink back at the snake.

"For I will pour water on the thirsty land, and streams on the dry ground; I will pour out my Spirit on your offspring, and my blessing on your descendants. They will spring up like grass in a meadow, like poplar trees by flowing streams. One will say, 'I belong to the LORD'; another will call himself by the name of Jacob; still another will write on his hand, 'The LORD's,' and will take the name Israel."
—Isaiah 44:3–5

*F*ather, pour out Your water on _____'s dry spirit. May my beloved child say, "I am the Lord's." May _____ call on the Lord and write on his hand, "Belonging to the Lord." You are _____'s Redeemer. Let my child say, "You are the Lord of hosts, and there is no God besides You." In Jesus's name. Amen.

◆ ◆ ◆

Torn and Silent

She rolls her eyes, and something like a grunt issues from her mouth. It seems as if anything I speak about comes through as nonsensical garble to her adolescent ears.

I remember fondly the times when all she could do was to ask me questions. "Why? How did God do that?" Back then, her eyes held my face in rapt attention for the wisdom she expected me to speak.

"What happened, Lord?" I ask. Sometime during her growing-up years, I underwent a metamorphosis, from wise to stupid. My words turned from teaching to insulting her intelligence. "What is a mother supposed to do? What can I say that will change her wayward heart?"

The sweet relationship we once held is torn. Its tattered edges wave in defiance of everything I taught her as a little girl. *Who is she now?* I find myself wondering.

But regardless of her attitude, I am her mother. The love for my little girl cannot be torn. I will wait for the time when my daughter begins to listen again. Time and maturity will mend our relationship. However, until then, I will wait to speak words of advice. My opinions will stay silent until she seeks them.

There is a time for everything, and a season for every activity under heaven: . . . a time to tear and a time to mend, a time to be silent and a time to speak.
—Ecclesiastes 3:1, 7

*L*ord God, grant me the wisdom to know when to speak to _____ and when to remain silent. Mend my relationship with _____ and help me to realize this period of time will not last forever. In Jesus's name. Amen.

◆ ◆ ◆

Crown of Glory

My daughter is too young. My baby girl has not graduated from school, but she is pregnant.

I stare at the flat tummy showing brazenly above the low-cut jeans. A diamond sparkles from her belly button, not her left hand. My concerns have proven valid. I had thought she might be sexually active, but she had sworn she was not.

I know my disappointment shadows my face as I reach out to hug her. Her tears wet my shoulders. Not tears of joy, but drops of shock and disbelief run down her young cheeks. I notice one hangs onto a small pimple. She is too young to have a baby; she should just be producing acne. My daughter did not think it could happen to her. Oh, the innocent pride of youth!

Well, we will see it through. I had always thought it would be fun to be a grandma—not this soon, but someday. Nevertheless, someday has arrived and my grandbaby's arrival is now only months away.

My daughter has made some mistakes, but I will not let her poor choices change my love for her or influence my relationship with this precious life growing inside of her. I will claim Psalm 103:17: *"But from everlasting to everlasting the LORD's love is with those who fear him, and his righteousness with their children's children."* I know the Lord's everlasting love will sustain my daughter, the newborn infant, and me. I choose my new grandchild to be my crowning glory.

Grandchildren are the crowning glory of the aged; parents are the pride of their children.
—Proverbs 17:6 (NLT)

*F*ather, grant _____ and me mercy and grace as we prepare for this new life. I pray that _____ will take pride in how I handle this situation. Help me to demonstrate Your love and righteousness to _____ and my new and glorious grandchild. In Jesus's name. Amen.

◆ ◆ ◆

Sibling Rivalry

They cannot stand the sight of each other. One son considers his brother to be a Goody Two-Shoes who can do nothing wrong. Mr. Goody Two-Shoes thinks his younger brother is an obnoxious, spoiled rebel who intentionally disrupts our family to get attention. Neither boy can speak a decent word to the other. They seem to despise one another.

Caught between the hatred of my two sons, I attempt to quell the storms of sibling rivalry. I endeavor to act as the family peacemaker. Sarcasm and contempt spew from the mouths of each boy in response to my suggestions of brotherly reconciliation. So much for the scriptural admonition of Romans 12:18: *"If it is possible, as far as it depends on you, live at peace with everyone."* The advice falls flat in the air charged with the animosity between my two sons, whom I love.

Sibling rivalry expands within the walls of my home. Yet I wait with anticipation for the day when my boys unite in love. I believe this will happen as it did with Jacob and Esau, two boys engaged in rivalry, but then committed to reconciliation: *"But Esau ran to meet Jacob and embraced him; he threw his arms around his neck and kissed him. And they wept"* (Genesis 33:4). Let it be soon, Lord!

> *"He told him, 'Your brother came home. Your father has ordered a feast—barbecued beef!—because he has him home safe and sound.'*
>
> *"The older brother stalked off in an angry sulk and refused to join in. His father came out and tried to talk to him, but he wouldn't listen."*
> —Luke 15:27–28 (*The Message*)

*O*h Father, help my older son realize that his younger brother needs love and compassion instead of going away in an angry sulk. Bring my younger son, _____, back into complete reconciliation in our family. Grant _____ the ability to understand the place of insecurity in which his older brother has placed himself. And Lord, help me as far as it is possible to live in peace with both of them! In Jesus's name. Amen.

◆ ◆ ◆

Show and Tell

He marched to the front of his kindergarten classroom. He proudly presented his daddy, clad in a sharp blue uniform: "This is my daddy. He's a police officer!" My son was so proud of his father. His daddy could do nothing wrong.

On Bring Your Child to Work Day, my son and I went to my work together. He sat quietly on a wooden stool as I helped people decipher their insurance policies. He heard big words such as liability, deductibles, and hazard insurance. He thought I was the smartest mommy in the world.

My son used to declare, "I am going to be a policeman when I grow up. And I am going to marry you, Mommy, because you're the prettiest woman ever."

However, something transformed mom's and dad's magnificence sometime between kindergarten and college. Our son no longer desires to be around us. He becomes angry if we suggest we meet his friends. We no longer have a mutual show-and-tell relationship with our son.

He wants nothing to do with us. How does this happen in a family? He embarrasses his father with his disrespect for the law. Why does he disobey everything we taught him? He grieves my heart with rudeness and sarcastic remarks.

I sometimes wonder, *Who is this man?* I do not know. Nevertheless, I am going to my Father God in prayer. I will show and tell Him about my wild child.

A foolish son brings grief to his father and bitterness to the one who bore him.
—Proverbs 17:25

My son, keep your father's commands and do not forsake your mother's teaching.
—Proverbs 6:20

*O*h Lord God, _____ brings grief to his/her father and bitterness to me. Help us to restore this broken relationship with _____. Let _____ remember and keep the commands of his/her father and not to forsake my teaching. I pray this in Jesus's name. Amen.

———— ◆ ◆ ◆ ————

Wilted Flower

Her father wilted the flowering spirit of our daughter. I watched the roots of my child's self-esteem dry up and wither away.

He scolded. "I don't want Bs. I want to see As." "Yes, you're thin, but you need to buff up." "Throw the ball! You throw like a girl."

He ridiculed. "You're so stupid you would show your backside to a dead bird." "You're so awkward; do you want to sign up for ballet?" "How come you can't get a boyfriend?"

After every weekend visit, she came home wounded by the sharp thorns of his words. I would nurse my little rosebud back to emotional health, but the scars remained.

As she grew up, she toughened up. She became everything her father demanded.

Now she struts with poise down the boulevards in spiked heels and hot pants. Her toned body, suntanned to a golden bronze, turns men's heads. Now she is street smart. My daughter makes a living out of showing herself to men.

It is Father's Day today. My little girl never knew the love of her father. She still searches for a daddy's approval. So I mailed *her* a Father's Day card with the imprint of the following Scripture:

> *"I will be a Father to you, and you will be my sons and daughters, says the Lord Almighty."*
> —2 Corinthians 6:18

I pray she takes the message to heart and understands she has a heavenly Father who loves her.

*Fathers, don't exasperate your children by coming down hard
on them. Take them by the hand and lead them in the way of
the Master.*
—Ephesians 6:4 (*The Message*)

$\mathcal{D}$ear Heavenly Father, heal _____'s emotional
wounds from the father who exasperated him/her. Take
_____ by the hand and lead him/her in Your way. Show
_____ that You are his/her true, loving, and accepting
Father. In Jesus's name. Amen.

◆ ◆ ◆

Send Someone

$\mathbb{M}$y child frightens people, sometimes even me. The surly expression
warns against attempting unwanted communication. The gothic
clothing advises caution in any interaction. The skull-and-crossbones
patch informs others of the poisonous personality underneath the
black leather jacket. The bulge in the front pocket suggests a possible
weapon.

No one dares to approach my child. Fear shows through their
downcast eyes. They hasten to avoid social contact. A safe distance
stands between my child and their apprehension. I understand. Even
I respond at times in trembling trepidation.

However, because of my prayers, I know the Lord Jesus beckons
someone to come to my child. The Holy Spirit will inspire someone to
befriend my child despite his or her fear. Someone will be obedient.
Someone will come.

*"But Lord," exclaimed Ananias, "I've heard about the terrible
things this man has done ..."*

But the Lord said, "Go and do what I say …."
So Ananias went and found Saul. He laid his hands on
him and said, "Brother Saul, the Lord Jesus, who appeared
to you on the road, has sent me so that you may get your sight
back and be filled with the Holy Spirit."
—Acts 9:13, 15, 17 (NLT)

*L*ord Jesus, I ask You to send someone to _____. I pray
for that someone to be like Ananias, obedient despite the terror _____
_____ produces when approached. Bless this someone who is willing to
reach out and touch _____. In Your name, I pray. Amen.

——————— ◆ ◆ ◆ ———————

Civil War

*S*he looked at me!" "He touched my leg!" "I *get* the front seat!" "No,
I *have* the front seat." "Mom!" I heard in rapid succession.

I used to sit in the minivan and wonder, *Why in the world did*
I want kids? It must have come from the silent row of baby dolls that sat
quietly on the shelf in my childhood bedroom. Those plastic children
always got along so well with each other.

"Get out of my room!" "I hate you!" "You have to be adopted; you
are not like us." "Just go to…" "Mom!"

The high school years with my children were like living in a war
zone. I felt like the secretary of state, running hither and thither
attempting to make peace between the warring factions of our home.
I tried for a peace treaty, but failed.

They are now adults and nothing has changed. My children despise
each other. Since my children are not Christ followers, there is no
motivation for reconciliation. They do not *want* the peace He can give;
they prefer civil war.

"If she is coming over for Thanksgiving, I won't be there."

"He's rude and obnoxious. I will not subject my kids to his vulgarity."
"Yes, they are my sisters, but they are both…"
"If I ever see him again, I'll knock the…."
"Oh, Mother!"

I weep over my family of prodigal children. In my lifetime, I want to experience the joy of being able to say, *"How wonderful, how beautiful, when brothers and sisters get along!"* (Psalm 133:1 *The Message*).

"Oh, Heavenly Father…!"

"If a kingdom is divided against itself, that kingdom cannot stand. If a house is divided against itself, that house cannot stand."
—Mark 3:24–25

*O*h Heavenly Father, my house is divided against itself. It cannot stand. Bring my children, _____, _____, _____, _____, and _____, to faith in Your Son, Jesus Christ. Grant them peace and reconciliation that can come only from You. In Your Son's name. Amen.

◆ ◆ ◆

Whispers of Relationships to My Wild Child

Dear Wild Child,

In Scouts, you learned to tie rope knots that would not, could not, become untied. Each type of knot with its own name: figure-eight knot, granny knot, manrope knot, and shroud knot. Each knot designed to hold together something by its particular design.

My child, relationships are held together by different types of ropes. Ropes knit together with strands of humility, gentleness, and patience. The relationships—tied with the knots of peace and love.

59

More times than I can count, our relationship has snapped with frayed emotions. Anger and frustration gnaw at our love for each other. Our relationship hangs by a thread.

I say, let's bury the hatchet. Let's choose to mend our parent-child relationship! It is our choice in how we deal with each other's faults. Let's put our misunderstandings and hurt feelings behind us. Let's begin a fresh knot of love to hold us together.

You were always a great knot-tying scout. I know we can do this together.

Be humble and gentle. Be patient with each other, making allowance for each other's faults because of your love. Always keep yourselves united in the Holy Spirit, and bind yourselves together with peace.
—Ephesians 4:2–3 (NLT)

𝓕ather God, teach _____ and me to be gentle and humble in our relationship. Help us to be patient with each other and to make allowances for each other's faults because of Your love. Always keep _____ and me united in the Holy Spirit. Bind us together with Your peace. In Jesus's name. Amen.

5

Whispers of Compassion

A New Day

"Why does the sun come up every day? How does it know when to shine?" These questions used to spurt from my four-year-old's inquisitive mind.

"Sweetie, because God tells the sun to shine each new day," I would reply. "Even when it is cloudy, the sun still shines. We just can't always see it."

Now, 20 years later, I think back to the innocence of those questions and the truth of the answers. The purity of my child disappeared into the dark oblivion of lasciviousness. But the Lord causes the sun to shine every morning, even when all I can see are the clouds of doubt and depression. From my human eyes, I cannot see a ray of sunshine in the future of my child.

However, the truth of God's Word tells me that His compassion for my child is new every morning. The Lord's great love for my child never fails, regardless of my child's indulgence in every type of adult immorality. So I remind myself, *The sun shines even when my heart's feelings cloud the view.* The Lord's faithfulness is great—yesterday, today, and tomorrow. Every day is a new day in the eyes of God and for the future of my child.

Because of the LORD's great love we are not consumed, for his compassions never fail. They are new every morning; great is your faithfulness. I say to myself, "The LORD is my portion; therefore I will wait for him."
—Lamentations 3:22–24

*O*h Lord, because of Your great love, _____ is not consumed, because Your compassions never fail. They are new every morning for _____. Great is Your faithfulness to _____. I pray, "The Lord is _____'s portion, therefore I will wait for You." In Jesus's name. Amen.

◆ ◆ ◆

An Abomination

They called my son an abomination. These same women had taught my child every week when he had been in Sunday School class. They had praised him for his Scripture memorization. Each of them, at one time or another, had told me that my son had the sweetest and kindest nature they had ever experienced in a little boy.

However, today my child has become an abomination in their minds. This clique of women has gathered around me to chide me for "allowing" my son to choose the gay lifestyle. Their eyes speak with malice. They urge me to sever my relationship with this reprobate.

Anger surges through my pain-filled thoughts. *How dare they? What do they know? Don't they realize he still possesses a sweet and kind nature? He is still my child!*

I choose not to retaliate with harsh words. It would not help them, my child, or me. Instead, I focus on how to respond to such religious piety. I wonder, *Where is your Christian compassion and kindness?*

"Thank you for your concern. Will you promise to pray for my family as we struggle with this insidious situation?" I ask with a lump in my throat. My pain lifts as I turn away, knowing I responded well. I feel God's nod of approval—*"Well done, good and faithful servant"* (Matthew 25:21).

> *Therefore, as God's chosen people, holy and dearly loved, clothe yourselves with compassion, kindness, humility, gentleness and patience.*
> —Colossians 3:12

*O*h Lord, help me to react with kindness and patience to others who harshly judge my child, _____. God, allow Your compassion and gentleness to invade the comments of others who feel they must give their opinion. Clothe us all with Your Spirit. In Jesus's name. Amen.

———————— ◆ ◆ ◆ ————————

Don't Cry

I keep the door to my son's room closed. My heart aches each time I attempt to dust or vacuum the vacated room. Old nursery rhymes rerun through my thoughts: *"Wynken, Blynken, and Nod one night, Sailed off in a wooden shoe...."* I begin to weep.

My heart mourns the death of the mother-son relational bond that once occupied this room. The grief overwhelms me, but I know the Lord Jesus sees my tears. Jesus's heart reaches out to me.

My son may be gone from the house, and he may not acknowledge me as his mother, but Jesus can renew my son's spiritually dead heart. Jesus's heart and hands are reaching toward my son's bitter and lifeless heart.

Yes, the Lord will one day bring my son back home to me. Until then, I keep the door to his room closed.

As he approached the town gate, a dead person was being carried out—the only son of his mother, and she was a widow. And a large crowd from the town was with her. When the Lord saw her, his heart went out to her and he said, "Don't cry." Then he went up and touched the coffin, and those carrying it stood still. He said, "Young man, I say to you, get up!" The dead man sat up and began to talk, and Jesus gave him back to his mother.
—Luke 7:12–15

*L*ord Jesus, I know Your heart reaches out to me. You see my tears. Lord Jesus, go to _____ and touch him. Say, "_____, get up and go back to your mother." Raise my relationship with _____ from the dead. In Your name, I pray. Amen.

◆ ◆ ◆

Ruins Recycled

*T*his week's recyclables sit dirty and discarded in the plastic bins in the driveway. They await a mammoth truck to rumble by, pick them up, and then reprocess them into usefulness again.

Hmmm. I wonder what my family refuse will become in the future?

My child requires a bit of recycling too. She needs to move from the sphere of uselessness to usefulness. Her life resembles a heap of rubble as a result of her devastating decisions and illicit exploits.

Yet the Lord God excels in restoration with deep compassion for those lost years. He says, *"I will repay you for the years the locusts have eaten"* (Joel 2:25). The locusts of sin may swarm over my child; however, the Lord can remove them. He holds the ability to repair and recycle the life of my daughter. He alone is capable of making her useful in His kingdom.

Until then, I place my child in the recyclable bin of prayer. I pray for the miracle of renewal and restoration of the ruins she has made of her life.

Hmmm. I wonder what my daughter will become in the future?

The LORD will surely comfort Zion and will look with compassion on all her ruins; he will make her deserts like Eden, her wastelands like the garden of the LORD. Joy and gladness will be found in her, thanksgiving and the sound of singing.
—Isaiah 51:3

*D*ear Lord, comfort _____ and look with compassion on all her ruins. Make _____'s life of waste become like the Garden of Eden. I pray that joy and gladness will be found in _____, with thanksgiving and the sound of singing. In Jesus's name. Amen.

◆ ◆ ◆

Ribbons and Rainbows

Black ribbons of depression surround my daughter. Where once brightly colored ribbons adorned her hair and tickled her neck, melancholy now hangs heavy on her slumped shoulders. Her unkempt appearance announces her dreary mood.

Unfortunately, her dejection arises because the feral days of rebellion have resulted in harsh consequences. My daughter has discovered the truth of Numbers 32:23: *"You will be sinning against the LORD; and you may be sure that your sin will find you out."* The harsh results of sin chased her down, and now life is difficult.

However, God's compassion arises over guilt and depression. He sets a rainbow in the sky as a reminder on rainy days that He exists and

65

is in control. My child needs to look up from the dire consequences to the colorful rainbow of God's mercy and compassion. He waits to place a rainbow ribbon in her day; she just needs to look up to Him.

In the meantime, my own motherly compassion longs to do something. I am going to buy her some exotic shampoo and conditioner for that dirty hair. And I will purchase some brightly colored ribbons to tie up her long hair. Maybe they will help lift her head enough for her to see the rainbow.

"I have placed my rainbow in the clouds. It is the sign of my permanent promise to you and to all the earth. When I send clouds over the earth, the rainbow will be seen in the clouds, and I will remember my covenant with you and with everything that lives."
—Genesis 9:13–15 (NLT)

*L*ord God, show _____ the rainbow You have placed in the dark clouds of depression that envelope her. Help _____ to see the sign of Your permanent promise to her and all the earth. Lord God, when the clouds come, show Your rainbow brightly to _____. In Jesus's name. Amen.

——————— ◆ ◆ ◆ ———————

Heart of Flesh

*S*he strides into the room with her attitude declaring, "I dare you!" Her strong will holds no empathy for others. My daughter rationalizes, "Hey, get over it. I did."

Her stoic attitude evolves from overcoming her physical disabilities. She blames God. Her bitterness and resentment evolve from her physical handicaps. She rails against the truth of Psalm 139:13: *"For you created my inmost being; you knit me together in my mother's womb."* She charges back with the accusation, "If God formed me, He created my body this way. I hate Him for the way I am." Then she quotes, *"Why did I not perish at birth, and die as I came from the womb?"* (Job 3:11).

My heart breaks for my daughter's heart of stone. She needs to allow herself to feel compassion for others and herself. My cold, hard daughter needs to know that God loves her, formed her, and that He holds a purpose for her life that includes her disability.

However, she will not discover that purpose until she allows her Maker to give her a heart of flesh.

> *"'I will give you a new heart and put a new spirit in you; I will remove from you your heart of stone and give you a heart of flesh. And I will put my Spirit in you and move you to follow my decrees and be careful to keep my laws.'"*
> —Ezekiel 36:26–27

*L*ord God, give _____ a new heart. Put a new spirit in _____. Remove the heart of stone and give _____ a heart of flesh. Put Your Spirit in _____ and help him/her understand Your love for him/her. Move _____ to follow Your decrees. In Jesus's name. Amen.

———————— ◆ ◆ ◆ ————————

Outcast

Blotchy sores cover my son's body. Each time I visit him, I see that He weighs less. The sallow skin warns that his health is failing rapidly. His disease, acquired immune deficiency syndrome (AIDS), causes symptoms painful beyond a person's capability to understand physically or mentally.

My son is not sure how he contracted it. He thinks a woman

passed it on to him during a one-night tryst. I suspect drug use with contaminated needles. However, it does not matter how he became infected—AIDS wars within his body. It appears AIDS is winning.

Prior to my son becoming ill with the deadly disease, I paid little attention to the news of the AIDS epidemic. I thought to myself, *Serves them right!* It would never strike *my* family. I felt we were immune to this type of tragedy. I soon discovered no one is immune to AIDS.

I also ascertained that a lack of compassion flourishes in our society for AIDS patients.

My child is now an outcast. He hesitates to respond with the truth when asked about his health. I understand the ridicule and scorn he experiences, because the gossip filters through to me. I choose to disregard the comments.

My Lord Jesus overflows with compassion for society's outcasts. As AIDS grips my son, I cling to the Son of God.

Jesus answered them, "It is not the healthy who need a doctor, but the sick. I have not come to call the righteous, but sinners to repentance."
—Luke 5:31–32

"'But I will restore you to health and heal your wounds,' declares the LORD, 'because you are called an outcast, Zion for whom no one cares.'"
—Jeremiah 30:17

ℒord God, restore _____ to spiritual health and heal _____'s wounds. Restore _____ to You because he/she is an outcast for whom few seem to care. In Jesus's name. Amen.

◆ ◆ ◆

Midnight Hike

When my son attended kid's camp, the midnight hikes were his favorite activity. The walks in the dark usually followed the blazing campfire where counselors told scary stories. My son thrilled to walking in the dark and jumping at each unknown crackling sound.

Then as my son grew older, he went to youth camp. The late-night strolls still won the prize for the best event, because he could hold hands with a cute girl. He protected her from scary noises in the woods. His first kiss occurred on a midnight hike.

Now my adult son still wanders in the night to find excitement. Years ago, he quit attending church functions of any type. He said, "They are *so* boring. I need excitement in my life."

A few of my wild child's thrills are being arrested for underage drinking, taking antibiotics for a sexually transmitted disease, and losing his license for drag racing.

My child took the wrong path. He is out on a midnight hike filled with real danger. Yet God sees my son's wayward heart and holds great compassion for him. The Lord might let him wander for a while, but His great compassion will not abandon him to the darkness of this world.

"Because of your great compassion you did not abandon them in the desert. By day the pillar of cloud did not cease to guide them on their path, nor the pillar of fire by night to shine on the way they were to take."
—Nehemiah 9:19

Dear Jesus, because of Your great compassion, do not abandon _____ in the desert of his/her sin. I ask that by day You guide _____ on his/her path. By night, Lord, shine on the way _____ is to take. In Your name. Amen.

The Holler of Guilt

My daughter crept back into the arms of Jesus. She confessed her sins, but the guilt remains. Guilt hollers at her soul daily. Sorrow of remorse still digs deep into her spirit.

I read to her various Scriptures each day, to assure her of God's forgiveness. *"For I [the LORD] will forgive their wickedness and will remember their sins no more"* (Jeremiah 31:34). The pressure of her guilt lifts momentarily, but comes back with a vengeance when something reminds her of her faithlessness to the Savior. She slumps back into doubt and insecurity. "How can I be forgiven?" she asks.

Regardless of how my daughter feels, her sins have been forgiven. His Word speaks truth and healing to the repentant soul. It may take time for my daughter to accept His grace, so in the meantime I will remind her of God's compassion.

I search my Bible and read Micah 7:19: *"Once again you will have compassion on us. You will trample our sins under your feet and throw them into the depths of the ocean!"* (NLT).

Oh, that's a good one! I'll offer the Word from without to soothe her distressed soul. Surely a combination of the Word with messages from the Spirit of God within her will silence that holler of guilt.

My guilt has overwhelmed me like a burden too heavy to bear.... O LORD, do not forsake me; be not far from me, O my God. Come quickly to help me, O Lord my Savior.
—Psalm 38:4, 21–22

Oh God, _____'s guilt has overwhelmed him/her. It is a burden too heavy to bear. Oh Lord, do not forsake _____; do not go far from _____. Come quickly to help _____. In Jesus's name. Amen.

Whispers of Compassion to My Wild Child

Dear Wild Child,

Ten tiny toes. A little upturned nose. Wispy fine curls. I will never forget those first moments of examining you, my newborn child. Then suddenly, a nurse whisked you away to be weighed, washed, and wrapped. Although I was worn out by your birth, my eyes and heart followed you and the nurse throughout the stark hospital room. My arms ached to cuddle you again.

Nothing has changed as you have grown into an adult. Even when you rebel against me, I long to hold you close, to fill your needs, to make things right in your life. My compassion flows toward you, my wayward child. You can never erase my love for you.

If possible, I would take on your pain as my own. I cannot, but Christ Jesus did. When He died on the Cross, the nails engraved you on the palms of His hands. So please know that my love and compassion cannot compare to the love Jesus holds for you.

I love you and gave you birth. Christ loves you and He will deliver you too. *"Call upon me in the day of trouble; I will deliver you, and you will honor me"* (Psalm 50:15).

We will not forget you; we wait with open arms engraved with love and compassion. We watch for your return.

With love and compassion,
Mom

> *"Can a mother forget the baby at her breast and have no compassion on the child she has borne? Though she may forget, I will not forget you! See, I have engraved you on the palms of my hands."*
> —Isaiah 49:15–16

*O*h Father, I cannot forget my wild child, _____. Compassion pours out for _____, whom I bore. Lord, let my child know that You will not forget. Let _____ understand that You engraved him/her on Your hands. In Jesus's name. Amen.

◆ ◆ ◆

6

Whispers of
Peace

The Mommy Gift

She had wrapped the box in plain construction paper. Crayon markings scribbled words of endearment: "Mommy, I love you!" I carefully unwrapped it. With the paper pealed away, I lifted the cardboard lid.

I stared in horror at the curled-up form of a tiny brown mouse wedged inside the tissue paper. *Ughhh!* Then relief flooded over me as I realized it was a ceramic knickknack—but very authentic looking.

My child's face looked anxiously to see if I liked it. She wanted to please me with the unusual gift. "Oh honey, it's so unique! Where did you find it?" I said and gave her a big hug.

As time marches on, Mother's Day still comes around yearly. My daughter no longer brings me gifts wrapped in construction paper. They come swathed in fancy paper, ribbons, and bows. Now beautiful bric-a-brac lie nestled in satin. However, my daughter no longer cares if her presents please me. She gives me gifts because of protocol.

My daughter busies her life with men, alcohol, and drugs. She searches for something to bring her lasting peace and happiness. Although tranquility eludes her, she continues the hunt.

I accept the "mommy gift" each year with the same words. "Oh honey, it's so unique! Where did you find it?"

She hurries out the door with a perfunctory kiss on my cheek. She seeks peace, but it eludes her. I need peace about my child. My heart is troubled and afraid for her. What will she substitute for the gift of peace today?

> *"Peace I leave with you; my peace I give you. I do not give to you as the world gives. Do not let your hearts be troubled and do not be afraid."*
> —John 14:27

*S*weet Jesus, leave Your peace on _____. I need Your peace too. Show _____ You do not give peace as the world gives, but You give lasting—eternal—peace. Help both _____ and me not to let our hearts be troubled and afraid. I ask this in Your precious name. Amen.

◆ ♦ ◆

The Committee

A committee of voices competes in my mind. They murmur advice. Each voice demands I follow its command on how to respond to my wayward daughter. I hear the words, the accusations, the bullying demands, and the subtle coercion.

Tough love! shout my angry thoughts.

Love and forgiveness, whispers my mother's heart.

Enabler, murmurs the heart of mercy.

Failure! accuses the voice of guilt.

Why, God? asks the spirit of doubt.

All through the day, I hear the committee in my head. At night, they wake me from fitful sleep to remind me that I need to do something about my beloved daughter. I listen closely, trying to determine the right course of action. But in the end, the voices continue to linger with no vote of confidence in a specific decision.

At times, I feel as if I am losing my mind. The sorrow of my heart grips my soul until I feel I cannot think straight or make a rational decision. The voices battle on.

Then a soft voice gently overrides the committee in my head: *"Be silent, and know that I am God!"* (Psalm 46:10 NLT). Suddenly, a blanket of stillness resides in my thoughts. The committee bows to the authority of the Living God.

How long must I wrestle with my thoughts and every day have sorrow in my heart? How long will my enemy triumph over me?
—Psalm 13:2

*L*ord God, how long must I wrestle with thoughts about _____. Every day my heart sorrows over the behavior of my child, _____. Come bring Your peace to my heart. Do not allow the voices of the enemy to triumph over me. In Jesus's name. Amen.

— ◆ ◆ ◆ —

Overflow

*T*hey said medication would help my child's condition. "Medication will help your child deal with the volatile emotional swings. The rage, anxiety, depression, and spontaneous reactions to others will diminish." A warning also was offered: "Your child's destructive anger could cause damage to others in and outside your family."

Duh! That is why I am standing in the psychiatrist's office. The school board required a full physical and mental examination after unending escapades of fury. So we will try the promise of anger management in a bottle.

It will only succeed if my child agrees (and remembers) to swallow the pill every day. However, my child often forgets, or worse, refuses stubbornly to adhere to the doctor's recommendation.

Nagging does not change my teen's mind. It only produces the response, "You can't make me. It's my life!"

Although I cannot physically force a pill down my child's throat, I can pray for another answer. I ask for a different type of anger management to infuse my child's spirit. I will pray for the Holy Spirit to overflow peace into the life of my beloved child. I will pray for my child to accept the prescription of the doctor and of God.

May the God of hope fill you with all joy and peace as you trust in him, so that you may overflow with hope by the power of the Holy Spirit.
—Romans 15:13

*L*ord Jesus, I ask that You fill _____ with Your joy and peace. Help _____ to learn to trust You. Allow the hope and power of the Holy Spirit to overflow in the life of my beloved child, _____. In addition, Lord, let my child realize the benefits of the medication too. In Your name, I pray. Amen.

———————— ◆ ◆ ◆ ————————

Amaze Me

The wind of willfulness tears through my home. Rapids of rebellion run rampant in my relationship with my child. Insomnia stalks me. I lie awake attempting to find a way to calm the storm's insurgence that threatens to destroy our lives. Peace eludes me.

I fear for my child. I know intellectually that Christ can change the most difficult of people, but my heart trembles. I need to be amazed by His power over evil and sin. I want to be amazed as were the people mentioned in Mark 1:27: *"The people were all so amazed that they asked each other, 'What is this? A new teaching—and with authority! He even gives orders to evil spirits and they obey him.'"*

My Jesus has the power. I wait while the wind of willfulness and rapids of rebellion rage through my child. But I know that peace will come to our home. The Master will say to evil elements in my home, "Quiet! Be still."

I wait to be amazed. I sleep in peace.

He got up, rebuked the wind and said to the waves, "Quiet! Be still!" Then the wind died down and it was completely calm. He said to his disciples, "Why are you so afraid? Do you still have no faith?"
—Mark 4:39–40

The men were amazed and asked, "What kind of man is this? Even the winds and the waves obey him!"
—Matthew 8:27

*L*ord Jesus, please rebuke the wind and raging waters of rebellion in _____. Let the storm subside in our family. Lord Jesus, I ask that You amaze me with Your power. I want to be so amazed that I can say, "He commands _____ and even _____ _____ obeys Him." In Your name. Amen.

◆ ◆ ◆

Earthquake Answers

An actual earthquake rattles my house. Bone china teacups fall from shelves to shatter on the tile floor. One decorative plaque tumbles off the bookcase, cracking the glass frame.

As I pick it up, I read the old Chinese proverb, "A bird does not sing because it has an answer. It sings because it has a song."

The truth of the saying strikes me. Regardless of the fact that I seem to have no answer to solve the problem of my wild child, I do, at least, have a song to sing—a song of peace, the peace that flows from God. This steady peace cannot be taken from me no matter what emotional earthquakes might result from the reckless rebellion of my child.

Friends have often inquired how my heart survives the daily upheaval of the revolt of a completely out-of-control child. I do not know. I can only quote from Philippians 4:7: *"And the peace of God, which surpasses all comprehension, will guard your hearts and your minds in Christ Jesus"* (NASB).

As I acknowledge God's peace and protection in my daily life, I realize that is the answer for my wild child also. Only when my child discovers the peace of Jesus Christ will the emotional earthquakes cease.

I stare down at the damaged plaque. I now have not only a song, but also an answer for my wild child and myself—the peace of God, which surpasses comprehension.

"Though the mountains be shaken and the hills be removed, yet my unfailing love for you will not be shaken nor my covenant of peace be removed," says the LORD, who has compassion on you.
—Isaiah 54:10

*F*ather God, even though the mountains shake and the hills tremble, I know Your unfailing love for _____ will not be shaken. Your covenant of peace will not be removed from _____ or any of my family. Lord, show _____ Your compassion for him/her and help this child of mine to discover Your peace. In Jesus's name. Amen.

◆ ◆ ◆

Teeter-Totter

Neighborhood parks rarely have teeter-totters anymore. They are probably too dangerous for children.

I recall straddling the long thin board with a girlfriend on the other end. The green-painted plank was centered on a post. One of us would push off with our feet and then up and down we would go. Up. Down. Teeter-totter. Up. Down. Teeter-totter. However, one person would get the idea to jump off, and *wham!* The other person would slam into the ground.

Unfortunately, my child teeter-totters between her faith and pleasures of this world. One day she walks with God on a mountaintop experience; the next day she plays in the mud of sin.

My child is not having fun on either side. She cannot stay on a "high" with God, because faith dictates a faithfulness through the mountaintops and valleys of her experience with God. She cannot truly enjoy her trespasses because of her guilt. *Wham!* Sin lets her down too. My daughter is a living example of the statement, "The most miserable people in the world are those who have one foot in the Bible and the other in the world."

I pray the teeter-totter of faith will be removed from my child's life. It is dangerous for her to play on. One time she could be seriously injured when she slams down on the side of her waywardness. Somehow, the post that holds the plank of faith needs to be eliminated. No highs. No lows. No teetering between God and sin. She just needs to learn to walk in faith on even ground.

If your sinful nature controls your mind, there is death. But if the Holy Spirit controls your mind, there is life and peace.
—Romans 8:6 (NLT)

Heavenly Father, prevent _____'s sinful nature from controlling his/her mind. I pray that the Holy Spirit will control

_____ so that he/she will have life and peace. In Jesus's name. Amen.

◆ ◆ ◆

Invisible Cape

My six-year-old would drag a large terry bath towel to the kitchen. He wanted to turn it into a superhero cape. I would lean over and latch it on with a sturdy safety pin. His little bare feet tromped out of the room, while his active imagination allowed him to believe he had suddenly become invisible.

Times change. Now his large, size-11 shoes tromp through the kitchen, while he acts as if _I_ am invisible. He refuses to acknowledge me. I am no longer the mommy who helps him fly, but the woman who drags him down with her nagging.

He is no longer a superhero, but a family villain who brings chaos to our home. We both wish we held an invisibility cape to keep us apart from each other.

Thankfully, I know a super-God. He will grant me a cape of peace that will allow me to rise above my relationship with my child. I just have to remember to bring Him my tear-stained towel of concern for my child. My Jesus can transform my son from villain to superhero. He holds an imperceptible cape of peace for my child too.

Do not be anxious about anything, but in everything, by prayer and petition, with thanksgiving, present your requests to God. And the peace of God, which transcends all understanding, will guard your hearts and your minds in Christ Jesus.
—Philippians 4:6–7

_P_recious Jesus, help me to not be anxious over _____, but in everything concerning _____, to present my requests to You with prayer, petition, and thanksgiving. I pray for Your peace, which transcends all understanding, to guard _____'s and my heart and mind. In Your name, I pray. Amen.

◆ ◆ ◆

Peace Porridge

Oatmeal steamed in the bowls. The flakey goop sprinkled with brown sugar and raisins and served with cold milk topped the list of breakfast favorites for my child. I think the old nursery rhyme that we sang over it added to the savory experience: "Pease porridge hot, pease porridge cold, pease porridge in the pot, nine days old..."

Now when I sit at the breakfast table, I do not sing "Pease Porridge" anymore; rather, I pray for a "peace portion" for my child. My daughter's mean-spiritedness leaves her and me without any peace. Testiness oozes out of her like the melted brown sugar spread across the morning oatmeal. Unfortunately, she lacks any of the sweetness.

I recognize her crankiness comes from a lack of tranquility within. The words of Jesus come to mind: *"Blessed are the peacemakers, for they will be called children of God"* (Matthew 5:9 NRSV). My child certainly would not be thought of as a child of God from other persons' perspectives. She is *not* a peacemaker.

However, I know that God, in His power, can change her. Only He can make pease porridge into peace porridge and fill her to the brim with sweetness and serenity. Lord, hear my morning prayer for my child, "Peace portion..."

But the wisdom that comes from heaven is first of all pure. It is also peace loving, gentle at all times, and willing to yield to others. It is full of mercy and good deeds. It shows no partiality and is always sincere. And those who are peacemakers will

81

plant seeds of peace and reap a harvest of goodness.
—James 3:17–18 (NLT)

*L*ord Jesus, let the pure wisdom that comes from heaven fill _____. Pour into _____'s hungry soul peace, gentleness, and the willingness to yield to others. Fill _____ with mercy, good deeds, and sincerity. Teach _____ to become a peacemaker so he/she will reap a harvest of goodness. In Your name. Amen.

◆ ◆ ◆

The Quietness Within

Winter brings quietness to the earth. No birds chirp. Skateboards, bicycles, and in-line skates hide in closets. Snow muffles the sound of barking dogs. People's footsteps slip by unnoticed, except for the silent prints in the snow.

Winter reminds me to quiet my soul. During other seasons of the year, I fret over my daughter's rash behaviors. Worry riddles my workday. Anxiety washes through my sleepless nights. Yet somehow when the cold weather comes, stillness enters my soul. The truth of Hosea 6:3 resonates in my heart: *"Let us acknowledge the LORD; let us press on to acknowledge him. As surely as the sun rises, he will appear; he will come to us like the winter rains, like the spring rains that water the earth."*

The stark barrenness of the earth covered by sparkling white snow reminds me that no matter what my child does, God is in control. Her life may look barren to me, but the Lord can make the Holy Spirit rain down on my wild child and reign in her life.

Yes, winter stirs quietness within me. I pray that by springtime my child will have a new spiritual life that is full of hope and peace.

But I have stilled and quieted my soul; like a weaned child with its mother, like a weaned child is my soul within me. O Israel, put your hope in the LORD both now and forevermore.
—Psalm 131:2–3

*H*eavenly Father, still and quiet my soul concerning _____, like a weaned child with its mother. Also, Lord still and quiet _____'s soul. Oh, I pray that _____ will put his/her hope in You now and forevermore. In Jesus's name. Amen.

◆ ◆ ◆

Whispers of Peace to My Wild Child

Dear Wild Child,

Do you remember when I used to say, "I was not meant to be your friend; I am your mother." That statement was true when you were a child growing up. Now that you are an adult. I would tell you, "I want to be your friend."

I look around at my girlfriends. They enjoy being around their children and vice versa. Many times adult children become their moms' best friends. I envy those moms. Yes, I am your mother, but now it is time to become friends.

I long for our relationship to be full of peace rather than full of discord. Proverbs 17:1 states my feelings: *"Better a dry crust with peace and quiet than a house full of feasting, with strife."* I know you feel the same way.

So, my dear child, are you ready to make up and to start a new type of relationship? I promise not to boss and nag you. Could we go to a movie? (I will even let you choose it!) It will be my treat, and I will buy the fragrant bucket of buttery popcorn. Or how about a homemade pepperoni pizza and a game? (I won't let you win!)

Perhaps you are not ready for your mother to become your friend.

However, let us start by making peace with each other. I want to be a part of your life and your children's lives.

I close this note with love as your mother and your friend.

Jonathan said to David, "Go in peace, for we have sworn friendship with each other in the name of the LORD, saying, 'The LORD is witness between you and me, and between your descendants and my descendants forever.'"
—1 Samuel 20:42

*O*h Lord, help me and _____ to say to each other, "Go in peace, for we have sworn a friendship with each other in the name of the Lord." Lord God, I ask that You be a witness between _____ and me and with all the children of my wild child, _____. In Jesus's name, I pray. Amen.

◆ ◆ ◆

7

Whispers of Freedom

Duct Tape

Men joke that anything can be fixed by a little duct tape. It sticks, seals, and seams broken and damaged items. Usually silvery gray in color, it stands out, boldly declaring the haphazard repair.

Duct tape restoration reminds me of my child's life—temporary fixes wrapped round and round throughout his life. Detention. Counseling. Medication. Education. All these provide a provisional repair of sin's damage in my child's life. They hold my son together for a brief time and rip loose during the next episode of his sinful behavior. All the benefits disband into a gooey pile of unresolved difficulties.

I know my wild child will only be set free from his prison of problems when he allows Jesus Christ to become his life renovator and freedom provider. Until that time arrives, I can only wait and watch as my child continues to swathe himself in human, duct-tape-like answers to problems that arise from sinful behavior. Thankfully, I know the One who will unwrap my child and set him free.

Unrolling it, he found the place where it is written: "The Spirit of the Lord is on me, because he has anointed me to preach good news to the poor. He has sent me to proclaim freedom for

*the prisoners and recovery of sight for the blind, to release the
oppressed, to proclaim the year of the Lord's favor"... and he
began by saying to them, "Today this scripture is fulfilled in
your hearing."*
—Luke 4:17–19, 21

*L*ord Jesus, preach Your good news to _____. Proclaim
freedom from sin to _____. Open _____'s
blind eyes to see the truth. Oh Lord, release my wild child from
the darkness of sin that holds him as a prisoner. Proclaim to
_____ Your favor. In Your name, I pray. Amen.

◆ ◆ ◆

Failed Test

The solemn counselor shook her head no. This translated to me that
my daughter had failed the drug test. It was the third time in three
months.

My daughter stared defiantly and shrugged her shoulders.

Obviously, she does not want to stop doing drugs. She does not care
that her teeth are browning and beginning to rot. She must not mind her
pockmarked cheeks that continue to worsen because she picks at them
when she is high on methamphetamines. It does not matter to her the
agony her disease also brings to those who love her, or that I have spent
thousands of dollars on drug rehab. My daughter loves her drugs more
than she hates the disastrous results of being stoned out of her mind.

However, I know it is for her freedom from drugs that Christ died
on the Cross. And even though I want to give up on her, I will stand
firm. I will battle her drug addiction until I see her set free from the
substance abuse that consumes her body, mind, and soul. I will not
relent. I will not give up on my daughter. She may fail the drug tests,
but Jesus Christ will not fail her.

*It is for freedom that Christ has set us free. Stand firm, then, and
do not let yourselves be burdened again by a yoke of slavery.*
—Galatians 5:1

*L*ord Jesus, it is for _____ that You died on the
Cross. Through the power of the Holy Spirit, I ask that You eliminate
_____'s desire for drugs. Help _____ to
stand firm when she is clean again. Keep her from the yoke of drug
slavery. In Your name, I pray. Amen.

———————— ◆ ◆ ◆ ————————

Prison Break

The heavy metal door clanged behind me. The dour security
guard led me into a small waiting room. It was my first time in a
prison constructed of mortar and bricks. The stale air suffocated any
remembrance of the spring weather that only minutes before filled my
mind with hopeful thoughts. *How in the world did I end up here?*

I heard another thud of a metal door, and in walked my son, dressed
in white prison garb. I detected slightly the smell of chlorine bleach.
His ashen face appeared gray next to the white collar, but his brown
eyes brightened as he saw me sitting in the straight-back metal chair.

"Hi, Mom."

I tried to speak, but the words stuck in my throat even as the tears
flowed freely down my cheeks.

"I'm OK, Mom," he stated in a shaky voice.

I nodded my head. Again, I wondered to myself, *How did we end
up here?*

For five years, this place will house my son. It will never be easy for
either of us, but I know that God can work in my son's life anywhere.
The Almighty God rocked the prison walls for Paul and Silas. Their
release came through the power of prayer.

My prayer will not be for the physical release of my son. (Although, I wish for that type of freedom too). But I will pray that God will shake the foundation of his thinking until he is free from sin. May the tough lessons he learns, confined in this brick and mortar institution, prevent him from ever engaging in sinful and illegal activities again.

Suddenly there was such a violent earthquake that the foundations of the prison were shaken. At once all the prison doors flew open, and everybody's chains came loose.
—Acts 16:26

*F*ather God, I ask that You break _____ free from the chains of sinful behavior. Teach _____ Your mighty power and provision as he serves out this prison sentence. Break loose the chains of sin that bind _____. In Jesus's name. Amen.

———————— ◆ ◆ ◆ ————————

No Chains

*W*ithout a vocal greeting, the rattle of chains announces my son's return from work. His metal links jangle from his wrists, his pants, and his eyebrow. They display the appropriate symbol of the emotional and spiritual chains that imprison him. My son wears his chains as a badge of honor to his rebellion.

In my mind, I visualize the scene of Marley's ghost in *A Christmas Carol.* Huge, clanking chains and money boxes portrayed Marley's bondage to money. His remorse for his earthly deeds haunted him and Scrooge. I long for my son to feel remorse and to return as the sweet boy I once knew. I want my son back. Now!

As my son heads up the stairs, the clanking fades.

I shove the image of the ghostly Marley out of my thoughts and assert the positive promise, *"The Lord is not slow in keeping his promise, as some understand slowness. He is patient with you, not wanting anyone to perish, but everyone to come to repentance"* (2 Peter 3:9). I will continue to pray for my son. I will use Scripture to plead his case. Regardless of whatever shackles dangle from my son's body and soul, God's Word is not chained,.

> *But God's word is not chained.*
> —2 Timothy 2:9

*F*ather, I believe that Your Word is not chained. Help me to remain patient when You appear to be slow in keeping Your promises. I know You are infinitely patient, not wanting anyone to perish or live in rebellion. This includes my beloved child, _____. In Jesus's name. Amen.

◆ ◆ ◆

Ollie, Ollie, All in Free

*O*llie, Ollie, all in free!" This cry would ring throughout the neighborhood as my children and their friends played "hide and seek." When the streetlights popped on, as the dusk turned into darkness, the kids all knew they could come out and be free. The game ended until the next evening.

My children would stumble into the house, hot, thirsty, and hungry after playing outdoors in the summer heat. They expected a drink of cool water, a hearty dinner, and a place to plop down in front of the TV before they went off to bed.

Now my wild child stays out late in the darkness of night. She hungers for excitement. My daughter thirsts for attention. She dresses to allure. She desires for men to seek her out. My daughter yearns for "It" to find her.

In her game playing, sins consequences capture her. Medical repercussions have already caught up with her. My daughter's reputation precedes her in social situations. My child is a prisoner of her wild ways.

Nevertheless, my daughter knows the Light of the world can set her free. Not only did she memorize, "Ollie, Ollie, all in free," she memorized Scripture. She knows who calls her out of darkness to give her streams of Living Water. Deep within her thoughts, John 8:36 is able to cry out to her in the darkness: *"So if the Son sets you free, you will be free indeed."*

"Say to the captives, 'Come out,' and to those in darkness, 'Be free!' "They will feed beside the roads and find pasture on every barren hill. They will neither hunger nor thirst, nor will the desert heat or the sun beat upon them. He who has compassion on them will guide them and lead them beside springs of water."
—Isaiah 49:9–10

*O*h, Lord God, say to _____, "Come out and be free!" Do not let _____ hunger or thirst; do not let the desert sun beat upon _____. Lord God have compassion on _____ and guide my child to springs of Your living water. In Jesus's name. Amen.

◆ ◆ ◆

Busybody Biddy

*M*y daughter is hooked on gossip. She spreads tales and tattles. She pries in people's affairs until they completely reject her. Six employers have fired her because she is a busybody biddy.

Her tongue controls every aspect of her life. It holds her in bondage. Wounding words, petty prattle, and backstabbing barbs have cost my daughter her friends and work. She is alone in her prison cell of meddling.

I feel the lock on the cell door is her low self-esteem and personal insecurity. Somehow, when she pokes around in people's lives, she feels important. She believes she has the upper hand in situations, though they flip against her. She loses the respect of others and her self-value.

My daughter must change her life ambition. Instead of being a busybody biddy, she needs to lead a life of quiet with respect. She is in need of the key of freedom found only in the hand of Christ. He approves of her. He loves and respects her. He will even listen to her chitchatting chaos without it harming others. He will renovate her from a busybody biddy to a self-assured daughter of the King who cares only about the work of building the kingdom of God.

Make it your ambition to lead a quiet life, to mind your own business and to work with your hands, just as we told you, so that your daily life may win the respect of outsiders and so that you will not be dependent on anybody.
—1 Thessalonians. 4:11–12

Lord Jesus, teach _____ to make it his/her ambition to lead a quiet life. Show _____ how to mind his/her own business. I ask that _____ work hard so that his/her daily life may win the respect of others. I pray that _____ will not be dependent on anyone but You. In Your name. Amen.

◆ ◆ ◆

Overdose

Today it almost ended. It was afternoon, and my son still had not come out of his bedroom since going to bed the night before. Finally, worried, I tapped on the wooden door. No answer. I tried the door handle. Locked. With my fist, I pounded again. No response.

Frantic, I ran to the kitchen drawer and grabbed the ice pick. I jabbed it through the pinpoint hole in the doorknob and popped open the lock. I threw open the door, and there lay my son across his bed. He was still fully clothed in a red plaid flannel shirt and grubby jeans.

I raced across the room to shake him. No response. I slapped his face. No reaction. His skin, tinged with blue, felt cool to the touch.

I seized the phone and dialed 911. A voice answered. Weeping, I told them my child had apparently overdosed—again. The faceless voice took the necessary information and, with a matter-of-fact tone, stated, "An ambulance is on the way."

I prayed. God responded. His comfort enveloped me even as I heard the sirens screeching toward our home. I prayed. The Lord answered. The paramedics rushed my son to the hospital where he is recovering. The emergency room physician said, "This was a close call."

Sick, scared, and humbled, my wild child has agreed to admit himself into an intensive drug treatment facility. I pray my son responds to the assistance he will receive there from doctors and staff. I pray my son will answer the call of the Lord and receive an overdose of the abundant life.

Lord, your discipline is good, for it leads to life and health. You have restored my health and have allowed me to live! Yes, it was good for me to suffer this anguish, for you have rescued me from death and have forgiven all my sins.
—Isaiah 38:16–17 (NLT)

Oh Lord, discipline _____, for it leads to life and health. Restore _____ to health and allow him/her to live.

Let _____ say to You, "It was good for me to suffer this anguish, for You have rescued me from death and have forgiven all my sins." In Jesus's name. Amen.

———————— ◆ ◆ ◆ ————————

Trump Card

Card games rule my son's life. The hearts, diamonds, clubs, and spades boogie through his mind continuously. He works during the day so he can gamble at night. He tapes poker tournaments on television so he can learn the tricks of the trade.

After he loses all his money, he comes home, switches on the computer, and plays endless card games against the unseen intelligence. He sits mesmerized by red and black squares that flip up and down with a toggle of the mouse. My child lives to play cards.

His social life is nil. Fast food fills his gut, so he has more time for his games. He avoids sleep because he prefers to sit hunched over the games all night. He owes creditors. He projects a slovenly appearance. He does not care about anything but winning the next hand of cards.

Thankfully, I know my God has a card up His sleeve. God's love endures forever and will outlast any obsessive fascination with cards and gambling. You see, God always holds the trump card—love that endures forever.

> *He remembered our utter weakness. His faithful love endures forever. He saved us from our enemies. His faithful love endures forever.... Give thanks to the God of heaven. His faithful love endures forever.*
> —Psalm 136:23–24, 26 (NLT)

Father in heaven, Your love endures forever for my child, _____. You understand _____'s utter

93

weakness. Save _____ from the enemy of obsessions with gambling and cards. I give thanks to You in heaven, for Your love endures forever for _____. In Jesus's name. Amen.

◆ ◆ ◆

Cover-up Girl

Her porcelain skin, full pouty lips, and midnight-black hair formulate the perfect magazine cover girl. She is a modern Snow White who charms the world with outward beauty, but underneath hides a poisonous attitude of superiority.

People do not like her. They talk behind her back: "If she's a Christian, then I don't want to be one." "I'm tired of hearing her talk about her faith and then stab someone in the back."

I have attempted to talk with her about it, but she does not get it. She uses people for her own benefit. She states, "Well, I'm a cover girl, and I am a Christian. How rare is that? They need to treat me with more respect since I am an ambassador for God. Anyway, God will forgive, because that is what He does best."

True, He will forgive her. However, as her mother, I would rather have Christ say to my Snow White, *"Well done, good and faithful servant!"* (Matthew 25:23).

Sadly, my daughter does not grasp the concept of true Christianity. She believes in being served, rather than serving others. The bondage of prestige chains my child to hurtful behaviors. Her belief that her cover-girl good looks outweigh her pitiable Christianity causes others to despise her and ignore her representation of our Savior.

For it is God's will that by doing good you should silence the ignorant talk of foolish men. Live as free men, but do not use your freedom as a cover-up for evil; live as servants of God.
—1 Peter 2:15–16

*L*ord God, it is Your will that _____ do good and silence the ignorant talk of foolish people. Teach _____to live in freedom, but not to use his/her freedom as a cover-up for evil. Let _____ live as Your servant. In Jesus's name. Amen.

_____ ◆ ◆ ◆ _____

Whispers of Freedom to My Wild Child

Dear Wild Child,

It will seem strange to hear the following words from your mother. However, I want you to know that the chains of sin that currently bind you had me bound. Here is the deal—sin is pleasurable. If it were not, who would sin?

I know the burn of alcohol as shooters slide down the throat and inhibitions glide away. Thrills of sexual adventure create the feelings of being special. Marijuana mellowness pushes out the concerns of the day.

Yes, sin is fun. But it also entices, enslaves, and chains a person to a life of untold ill consequences. That is my whisper to you, my wild child. Consequences of my own wild ways still haunt me today. Although the chains of waywardness have long been broken, they still leave a trail of trouble.

Do not make the same mistakes your parent made. Learn from my harsh lessons. You have known me only as your mom and as a follower of Christ. Nevertheless, my history chronicles more than your memories about me.

Sweet child, choose to follow the way I now follow—the way of Christ. Allow Jesus to set you free from the enticement of sin's pleasure. Avoid the future results of poor choices today. Choose Jesus Christ. He will be good to you and grant rest for your soul—today and tomorrow.

Be at rest once more, O my soul, for the LORD has been good to you.... O LORD, truly I am your servant; I am your servant, the son of your maidservant; you have freed me from my chains.
—Psalm 116:7, 16

*O*h Lord, let _____ be at rest in his/her soul because You have been good to _____. Lord, I truly am Your servant. Please encourage _____ to learn to be Your servant too. Lord, You free me and _____ from our chains of sin. Thank You. In Jesus's name. Amen.

◆ ◆ ◆

8

Whispers of Truth

Lie Detector

The college dorm resembles a gypsy camp. A collage of information is strewn throughout the rooms, dining area, and the student union. Eclectic posters declare various political and philosophical opinions in an attempt to sway the new students. Advertisements for bars, rock concerts, and parenthood planning entice students to join in the freedom of campus life. This is the barrage of new information that has greeted the eyes of my child.

My child came home after one semester, strutting some of the new information she had picked up.

"I'm a vegan now."

A what? I thought, but kept my mouth closed.

"My professors say Christianity is a myth and that I have been duped by a hypocritical church."

"Honey, your dad is the pastor. You know we are not hypocrites in our faith," I responded with a lump of fear growing in my heart.

"Well, Dr. Smith proved in class that all religions are just a crutch for people who can't cope with life. There *is* no absolute truth. Anyway, even if there is a God, all paths would lead to him.

"Oh, and by the way, I don't eat eggs anymore—in anything. It's inhumane," my child declared with a voice of superiority.

I stood silent, watching my child strut out of the house. The door closed with a solid bang, as my spirit responded: *Oh yeah? Well, Jesus is the Way, and the Truth, and the Life. And no one comes to the Father except through Him!*

I headed for the rocking chair, my place of prayer. *Regardless of the lies my child hears at college, I will ask for a lie detector to engage in my child's spirit. I will pray against the subtle forces that influence my child's inquisitive mind. I will pray John 8:32 over my child: "You will know the truth, and the truth will set you free."*

As I settled back into my prayer chair, I made a mental note—no eggs. I will choose my battles. I will wage war against the spiritual lies, not insignificant issues.

Jesus answered, "I am the way and the truth and the life. No one comes to the Father except through me."
—John 14:6

*J*esus, open the mind of _____ to detect the lies. Give _____ the ability to realize You are the Absolute Truth. Remind _____ of Your faithfulness in our lives. Keep _____ free from lies. In Your name. Amen.

———————— ◆ ◆ ◆ ————————

Corsets and High Heels

A lacy black corset shoved up my daughter's cleavage. The spiked, red high heels made her legs appear muscular, yet slender and enticing. Her belly button sported a diamond loop that dangled against her toned abdomen.

I sat in shock and dismay before my girlfriend's computer. Incomprehensible images of my daughter floated on the screen before my eyes. *Who is this girl, and what has she done with my daughter?* This tantalizing tease on at a popular Web site community was not the same child that came to kiss *me* good night each evening.

Obviously, I had been duped completely by my teenage daughter's charm. Up until this day, I had seen her as a little girl still, dressed in the tulle of a pink princess, not lace lingerie. The diamonds in my mind's eye were mounted in a fake tiara, not sparkling in body piercings. Red sequined slippers belonged only in her storybook, *The Wizard of Oz.*

Well, that day was an eye-opener for this mom. I supposed my daughter felt herself invincible with her beauty and sexual allure closeted away from her mother's "dull" awareness. *Hmmm. ... I believe we will clean out her room together and toss those "costumes" she struts so brashly before a camera's lens,* I thought. *And those ruby red slippers— well, I just think we will send them back to Oz where they belong.*

Your beauty should not come from outward adornment, such as braided hair and the wearing of gold jewelry and fine clothes. Instead, it should be that of your inner self, the unfading beauty of a gentle and quiet spirit, which is of great worth in God's sight.
—1 Peter 3:3–4

*O*h, Father God, let _____ understand that her beauty should not come from outward adornment, such as braided hair, gold jewelry, corsets, and high heels. Instead, teach _____ that her inner self should display the unfading beauty of a gentle and quiet spirit, which is of great worth in Your sight. Let _____ somehow understand this truth, regardless of what our culture dictates. In Jesus's name. Amen.

◆ ◆ ◆

The Two-Step

Today my son went to church. Yesterday he came home stoned on marijuana. Tomorrow my son might witness to his best friend about God. The day after that, my son might land himself in the juvenile detention center. He does a two-step dance between faith in Christ and peer-pressure escapades.

Some days, my son's eyes glisten with the excitement of serving the Lord God. On other days, his glazed eyes see only worldly excitement, pleasure, and instant gratification. He desires both. My son fails to realize he cannot waiver between faith in God and the false gods this world offers. He refuses to reconcile the illogical dance of this ideology.

I watch him pursue the false god of pleasure. He sings and dances with the tune of temptation with no lasting satisfaction. He resembles the Israelites: *"Then they called on the name of Baal from morning till noon. 'O Baal, answer us!' they shouted. But there was no response; no one answered. And they danced around the altar they had made"* (1 Kings 18:26). The Israelite people danced with indecision between the Lord God and Baal.

I must be like Elijah. I will pray for my son today. I will challenge him with truth tomorrow. And perhaps soon, my son will stop the two-step of faith and declare, *"The LORD—he is God! The LORD—he is God!"* (1 Kings 18:39).

> *Elijah went before the people and said, "How long will you waver between two opinions? If the LORD is God, follow him; but if Baal is God, follow him."*
> *But the people said nothing.*
> —1 Kings 18:21

Lord God, show Yourself mighty in the life of _____.
Show _____ that the false gods of this world cannot offer

lasting satisfaction. Give _____ the courage to walk away from peer pressure and to dance into Your arms. In Jesus's name. Amen.

◆ ◆ ◆

The Craft Fair

Cloth dolls, pottery, and jewelry clutter the aisles of the huge indoor craft fair. The smell of homemade fudge, sandalwood incense, and grilled hot dogs mingle together, creating an indistinct aroma. People shove to reach the most coveted trinkets. Baby strollers block pathways as young mothers stop to chat.

This arena of homemade artistry displays the work of its crafty owners. By day's end, these artisans will achieve their wished-for monetary rewards. Their wares will be touted as objects of crafty success.

My child is "crafty," too, in the negative denotation of the word—filled with the intent to deceive others. My child delights in lies, schemes, and the other deceptive arts. My child preys upon the emotions of the intended victim. Then, when the unsuspecting prey takes the proffered bait, my child swoops in with the swindle. Embezzlement and fraud hide in my child's shadow.

Humiliation stalks me as the mother. I am at a loss for words to console the individual my child has intentionally harmed. Law enforcement watches my house, waiting for my child in the dark, to no avail. My cunning child knows not to show up at my home, for I would be the first to call the police.

My home is no place for that craftiness; this place is secure in the Holy Spirit who will convict my child of the wily ways, and comfort my broken heart.

He thwarts the plans of the crafty, so that their hands achieve no success. He catches the wise in their craftiness, and the schemes of the wily are swept away.
—Job 5:12–13

*L*ord, thwart the plans of _____ so that _____'s hands achieve no success. Catch _____ in that craftiness and illegal schemes. If necessary, use law enforcement to sweep away the wiles of my child, _____. In Jesus's name. Amen.

———————— ◆ ◆ ◆ ————————

Corrupt and Bankrupt

Television's criminal dramas imitate the reality of my son's life. Corruption trails his every activity involving money. My child thrives on deceiving others. He draws no boundaries in his fraudulent behaviors. Friends and family are fair game too.

Although my son accumulates immense wealth, his life is bankrupt. Betrayed friends yield loneliness. His deceit hinders the family's ability to welcome him with open arms. He is corrupt and failed.

I wait for my child to yield to Jesus; like Zacchaeus did, who was so far out on a limb that all he could do was fall into the waiting arms of Jesus (Luke 19:4). My child needs open eyes to the real truth: this world's wealth does not compare with the riches found in God's kingdom. Jesus, the Son of Man, is waiting to state about my crooked and bankrupt child, *"Today salvation has come to this house"* (v. 9).

But Zacchaeus stood up and said to the Lord, "Look, Lord! Here and now I give half of my possessions to the poor, and if I have cheated anybody out of anything, I will pay back four times the amount."

Jesus said to him, "Today salvation has come to this

house.... For the Son of Man came to seek and to save what
was lost."
—Luke 19:8–10

*D*ear Lord Jesus, give _____ the courage to stand up
and say, "Look, Lord! I will give to the poor and pay back anyone that
I have cheated." Lord Jesus, bring _____ to the point of
accepting Your salvation, for _____ is lost, and You came
to seek and to save the lost. I pray this in Your name. Amen.

◆ ◆ ◆

Issues

Conversations often buzz with the term. We state blithely, "Oh, she
has issues." Or "I have issues with that." Issues inundate our lives.

Issues ooze from my daughter's life too. Alcohol inhibits her
abilities. Drugs inhabit her lifestyle. For years, I have watched my child
sink lower into a pit of problems. She resists seeking help because of
shame and guilt. My daughter realizes she has messed up her life. She
believes any potential for change has disintegrated with her continuous
mistakes. Moreover, the alcohol and drugs continue to bamboozle the
will to change.

The woman in Matthew 9 dealt with her *"issue of blood"* for 12
years and then she discovered the courage to reach out and touch Jesus.
My daughter does indeed have issues, but she can also be made whole
by Jesus's power.

And, behold, a woman, which was diseased with an issue of
blood twelve years, came behind him, and touched the hem of
his garment: For she said within herself, If I may but touch his
garment, I shall be whole. But Jesus turned him about, and
when he saw her, he said, Daughter, be of good comfort; thy

103

faith hath made thee whole. And the woman was made whole from that hour.
—Matthew 9:20–22 (KJV)

*L*ord Jesus, _____ has issues. I ask for _____ to have the courage to touch You, even if it is the hem of Your garment. Let _____ know that You alone can make her whole with Your miraculous power. I ask that my child hear You say to her, "Be of good comfort; your faith has made you whole." I pray this in Your name. Amen.

◆ ◆ ◆

Fairy Tales

As a youngster, my daughter adored fairy tales. The good and evil intrigued her as she listened closely while I read to her. When I finished with, "And they lived happily ever after," she would sigh with relief and contentment.

My daughter still enjoys fairy tales—not the tales of Aesop and Brothers Grimm, but lies about her purpose in life. The New Age culture entices her with crystals and astrology to guide her through the day. She speaks to me of "channeling" with spirits and "astro travel." Her trancelike statements ring of subcultural brainwashing.

However, her eyes speak the truth. I detect a hollowness. She is not living the "happily ever after."

I beg her to come to church with me, but she refuses. When questioned whether she is a follower of Christ, alarm emits from her. She refuses to reply. *Has this subculture threatened her?* I wonder to myself.

So I pray for the fairy tales to dissolve, and I recite, *"But when he, the Spirit of truth, comes, he will guide you into all truth"* (John 16:13).

My wayward daughter will not find hope and happiness until she rejects the lies and accepts God's divine purpose for her life. Then, in the end, she *will* live happily ever eternally.

> *The lines of purpose in your lives never grow slack, tightly tied as they are to your future in heaven, kept taut by hope. The Message is as true among you today as when you first heard it. It doesn't diminish or weaken over time.*
> —Colossians 1:5 (*The Message*)

*F*ather, reveal to _____ that You have a purpose for his/her life. Place hope in my child's soul. Teach _____ that Your Message is as true today as when he/she first heard it. Let _____ know that it does not diminish or weaken over time. In Jesus's name. Amen.

◆ ◆ ◆

Pirate's Treasure

My son worships the treasures of this earth, and I do not mean the treasures earth's nature provides, such as midnight stars soaring, woods whispering, and seas singing. He treasures mutual funds, bonds, and precious metals. He specializes in the stock market trove.

Retirement reserves and investment interests of others entice my son to wheel and deal. He deliberately misleads people to trust his "brilliant" investment strategies. He coaxes capital from others, so he can use it to increase his own portfolio. He buries the treasures in a trail of useless paperwork, so that unsuspecting investors will never solve the puzzle of where their money disappeared. My wild child is a modern day pirate.

He thinks like the wily Jack Sparrow in *The Pirates of the Caribbean* movie. Pirates cheat other people. That is what they do. When I ask about his honor, my son grins and quotes Captain Sparrow, "Pirate!"

My son fears losing his riches. Gold and silver interlace a chain of greed that binds his integrity. He cheats others to provide a treasure for himself. The truth of Matthew 6:21 reflects my son's spiritual condition: *"For where your treasure is, there your heart will be also."*

However, Jesus loves my child. He asks him to shovel out from dependence on his financial portfolio—his pirate's treasure. At this time, my son walks away. Yet I know Jesus waits in love for my wild pirate to return with an open heart to find true treasures.

> *Jesus looked at him and loved him. "One thing you lack," he said. "Go, sell everything you have and give to the poor, and you will have treasure in heaven. Then come, follow me."*
> —Mark 10:21

*D*ear Jesus, look at _____. I know that You love _____. Help _____ to understand what he/she lacks. Reveal to _____ the importance of a treasure in heaven. I pray that _____ begins to follow You. In Your name, amen.

◆ ◆ ◆

Spittle

*W*hy do athletes spit? Do they have a bitter taste in their mouth? Does it make them feel rough and tough?

At high school sport events, I have observed both guys and girls pucker and then discharge a slimy slew. It disgusts me. If my foot accidentally slides on top of it, that repulses me.

Sadly, I think this is how the Lord Jesus feels about my child and his faith. He claims to be Christian, but no one would ever know. He strolls through life with a nonchalant attitude of noncommittal toward God.

Yet, because the Father loves my indifferent child, He will react in love and truth. The Father might rebuke and discipline him. My son may receive a "spiritual spanking" to guide him back to a place of passionate faith. And that is OK by me, because I detest spit, and I do not want my son to become spittle in the mouth of the Lord God.

> *"I know your deeds, that you are neither cold nor hot. I wish you were either one or the other! So, because you are lukewarm—neither hot nor cold—I am about to spit you out of my mouth. You say, 'I am rich; I have acquired wealth and do not need a thing.' But you do not realize that you are wretched, pitiful, poor, blind and naked.... Those whom I love I rebuke and discipline. So be earnest, and repent."*
> —Revelation 3:15–17, 19

$\mathcal{L}$ord Jesus, You know the deeds of _____. He/she is neither cold nor hot. Change the heart of _____ from being lukewarm to passionately in love with You. Because You love _____, I believe You will rebuke and discipline him/her. Lord, I pray that _____ will be earnest and repent. In Jesus's name. Amen.

◆ ◆ ◆

Whispers of Truth to My Wild Child

Dear Wild Child,

Tests are a part of life. You do not test well for school exams. Tryouts for sporting events stress you out. You failed your first driver's test because of nerves. Tests stink, don't they?

Several years ago at a youth event, you accepted Christ as your Savior. I watched your life change from good to great as you allowed Jesus to teach you the truth of God. Then somewhere, you strayed from the Teacher.

Do not allow feelings of failure to keep you away. The Lord Jesus knows how easy it is to become distracted in the school of faith. He taught his twelve disciples, whose minds wandered. They were distracted by money, busyness, and life in general. Yet Jesus persevered in teaching them the truth.

Whether or not you realize it, the Lord is persevering with you too. My dear child, will you allow the Lord to test you and show you where you are failing in your walk of faith? God loves you. He wants you to pass. Will you take the following exam from Psalm 139?

> *Investigate my life, O God, find out everything about me; Cross-examine and test me, get a clear picture of what I'm about; See for yourself whether I've done anything wrong— then guide me on the road to eternal life.*
> —Psalm 139:23–24 (*The Message*)

No need to fret. God will give you an A for the inquiry of truth. Tests are a part of life—eternal life.

> *Test me, O LORD, and try me, examine my heart and my mind; for your love is ever before me, and I walk continually in your truth.*
> —Psalm 26:2–3

*D*ear Lord, test and try _____. Examine _____'s heart and mind. Show _____ that Your love is ever before him/her. Teach _____ to walk continually in Your truth. In Jesus's name. Amen.

◆ ◆ ◆

9

Whispers of Conversations

Intimate Conversation

Tight-lipped, my wild child refuses to enter into a conversation. But my child's body language speaks without any words. His arms crossed, his back stiff, his head turned, he sits in complete defiance.

He will not share with anyone why he behaves with total rebellion to any authority. I try to coax answers from him with a mother's love that almost smothers. Counselors prod in an attempt to resolve the conflict. Even friends try to break down the barriers and enter into a deeper level of communication, but to no avail. My son evades any type of intimate conversation. His thoughts hide behind block walls of silence.

Whatever thoughts he wants to share—he acts out in rebellious behaviors. He mocks me. He snubs the therapists. He ridicules the friends who attempt to talk about anything of personal importance.

However, God knows my child's innermost considerations: *"You know when I sit and when I rise; you perceive my thoughts from afar"* (Psalm 139:2). Therefore, even though my rebellious wild child will not talk to anyone, I know God hears him. And more importantly, the Spirit can speak to my son. Hallelujah!

You can tell for sure that you are now fully adopted as his own children because God sent the Spirit of his Son into our lives crying out, "Papa! Father!" Doesn't that privilege of intimate conversation with God make it plain that you are not a slave, but a child? And if you are a child, you're also an heir, with complete access to the inheritance.
—Galatians 4:6–7 (*The Message*)

*H*eavenly Father, allow _____ to know that he/she is Your creation—Your child. You sent the Spirit of Your Son to come into his/her life so that _____ would cry out "Papa! Father!" Make it plain to _____ that he/she can belong to and have intimate conversations with You. Let _____ recognize that he/she is can be an heir to Your kingdom. In Jesus's name. Amen.

◆ ◆ ◆

They Said...

They said my child was worthless. They said my child would never amount to anything. They said my child was not welcome at our church.

My wild child left with bitterness and disappointment. She left, feeling the sting of rejection from the people who had taught her about the love of God. The Sunday School teachers, who memorized Scripture with her, now ignore my child. The church friends, who celebrated holidays with us, now refuse to associate with her. Her Christian pals who wear the "What would Jesus do?" bracelets reject her. They have all discarded my daughter because of her lifestyle.

Thankfully, the Son of Man, Jesus, does not reject the person whose life is steeped in sin. Instead, Jesus seeks that wild child, who is blinded by sin, and He opens that person's eyes. Then He engages that wild child with conversations of compassion and truth. Gratefully, Jesus does not pay any attention to what *"they said."* He converses in love and forgiveness: "Take heart, My wild child; your sins are forgiven."

They said, "You're nothing but dirt! How dare you take that tone with us!" Then they threw him out in the street.
Jesus heard that they had thrown him out, and went and found him. He asked him, "Do you believe in the Son of Man?"
The man said, "Point him out to me, sir, so that I can believe in him."
Jesus said, "You're looking right at him. Don't you recognize my voice?"
"Master, I believe," the man said, and worshiped him.
—John 9:34–38 (*The Message*)

*L*ord Jesus, close my _____'s ears to what "they" said. Jesus, You know they asked _____ not to step inside our church. Please Lord, go and find _____. Ask _____ to listen to and recognize Your voice of love instead of what they said. Lord, I ask that my child, _____, will believe and worship You. In Your name. Amen.

———————— ◆ ◆ ◆ ————————

Truth or Dare

*A*t age two, my child stated one word with emphasis: "No!" Even when she wanted to say yes, an independent, "No!" came sputtering out of her little rosebud mouth. We all laughed. Everyone thought it was cute—at the time.

It is not endearing now. My child argues on every single issue. Her irritable attitude and challenging tone dare me to disagree. She goads me to differ with her, no matter what the topic.

"White"—"Black"
"Republican"—"Democrat"
"Jesus"—"Buddha"
"Christian"—"Atheist"
"Purity"—"Unholiness"

Her freckled nose turns up at the slightest hint of speaking truth to me. I can only differentiate truth as what would be the complete opposite of what my daughter states. I dare her to speak the truth. She responds with the body language of a closed door.

My frustration builds as my hope dwindles. This season of adolescence is worse than the perpetual no of the two-year-old. Will she ever grow up in Him?

Although my daughter may continue to challenge me, with God's help, I will speak the truth to the best of my ability.

Show me your ways, O LORD, teach me your paths; guide me in your truth and teach me, for you are God my Savior, and my hope is in you all day long.
—Psalm 25:4–5

*D*ear God, show _____ Your ways. O Lord, teach _____ Your paths; guide _____ in Your truth and teach him/her, for You are God his/her Savior, and our hope is in You all day long. In Jesus's name. Amen.

———————— ◆ ◆ ◆ ————————

Potty Mouth

My daughter spews profanity. It shocks all those who hear her. Her soft, pink lips do not seem capable of uttering curses, damnations, and foulness. Yet not a sentence comes forth without her using God's name in a derogatory manner.

Where has she learned these phrases? How could my little girl talk like a reprobate? I am not sure I even know what some of the words imply that she uses so freely. (And I probably do not want to know.) What happened to her memorization of the Ten Commandments— specifically, the commandment, *"No using the name of GOD, your God, in curses or silly banter; GOD won't put up with the irreverent use of his name"* (Exodus 20:7 *The Message*)?

Shock and dismay fill my heart. I imagine washing out her potty mouth with a bar of soap, but that would not clean up her inner attitude and its foul results. I realize that I must wait for God to appear in His Holiness and reprove her Himself. The picture of the prophet Isaiah comes to mind:

I said, "Doom! It's Doomsday! I'm as good as dead! Every word I've ever spoken is tainted— blasphemous even!..." Then one of the angel-seraphs flew to me. He held a live coal that he had taken with tongs from the altar. He touched my mouth with the coal and said, "Look. This coal has touched your lips. Gone your guilt, your sins wiped out."
—Isaiah 6:5–7 (*The Message*)

That would do it! I will pray for God to convict my foul-mouthed child.

"A good person produces good deeds from a good heart, and an evil person produces evil deeds from an evil heart. Whatever is in your heart determines what you say."
—Luke 6:45 (NLT)

*D*ear Lord, I want _____ to be a good person who produces good deeds from a good heart. Lord, show _____ the evil in her mouth. Change the heart of _____ to express goodness and respect for Your name. I pray in Your holy name. Amen.

———————— ◆ ◆ ◆ ————————

Peer Pressure

The purple-spiked hair clashed against green eye shadow. The weight of her earrings threatened to rip her delicate earlobes. Other rings protruded from under her yellow cashmere sweater. Both sets of rings swung to the pounding of the music that issued forth from the dangling digital player.

As I watched her bebop up the stairs, I tried to remember what she looked like before she grew into an adolescent. Only a vague recall of a pixie face flitted across my mind. Peer pressure had changed my daughter. As each year had passed, she had become more consumed by what others thought about her. To be accepted by her peers, she caved in to ludicrous behaviors. If her friends did it, so did she—regardless of the pain of the procedure.

I try to advise and caution, but who am I? I paraphrase James 2:1 (*The Message*): "My dear child, don't let public opinion influence how you live your life." But I am only her mother.

"You're old-fashioned. You just don't understand me," she throws out and rolls her eyes. She pops the earplugs back into ears to "jam" to the music of her world—the world I am not a part of anymore.

Peer pressure wins for today. Soon my daughter will mature to adulthood. Then her friends' influence may slacken its grip. She will realize that her old-fashioned mother might have a few tidbits of wisdom to share.

Am I now trying to win the approval of men, or of God? Or am I trying to please men? If I were still trying to please men, I would not be a servant of Christ.
—Galatians 1:10

Father, teach _____ not to try to win the approval of her friends. Help _____ not to cave in to cultural conformity. Show _____ the value of learning to please You. I ask, as

114

her mother, that _____ will desire to be a servant of Christ, not a slave to peer pressure. In Jesus's name, I pray. Amen.

◆ ◆ ◆

Deep Silence

I woke to silence. No demands for breakfast floated down the stairway. The frantic question, "Where are my shoes?" did not filter through the air vents. Silence filled the house.

We argued. The fight escalated from shrill accusations to shoves. She shoved me; I pushed back. Then my daughter slapped me.

"That's it. Get out!" I said with finality.

"Don't worry. I'm out of here!"

She packed a bag and left. I have not heard from her since. Where she is staying is anybody's guess. Remorse envelopes my thoughts. *How could have things gotten so out of hand? And I am supposed to be a Spirit-filled woman!*

Although she has become a brat, I know she regrets the scene too. However, her pride will not let her return home.

So we linger in deep silence apart from each other, feeling downcast in our souls. Mother and child disturbed by our own behaviors, yet not knowing how to reconnect.

Thankfully, she *knows* I love her. And I believe she loves me. I must put my hope in God. He is the God of reconciliation. He will reunite our hearts with peace. I vow calmness will be the tenet of our home—not roaring waves of anger.

Deep calls to deep in the roar of your waterfalls; all your waves and breakers have swept over me.... Why are you downcast, O my soul? Why so disturbed within me? Put your hope in God, for I will yet praise him, my Savior and my God.
—Psalm 42:7, 11

115

$\mathcal{G}$od, call deeply to _____. Let _____ hear the roar of Your waterfalls. Let all Your waves and breakers sweep over _____. Enable _____ to question, *"Why are you downcast, O my soul? Why so disturbed within me?"* Help _____ to put his/her hope in You and praise You as his/her Savior and God. In Jesus's name. Amen.

———————— ◆ ◆ ◆ ————————

Forked Tongue

My son should claim the title, "Master of Deceit." He lies constantly consistently twisting in strands of truth. He speaks flattery to persuade. He exaggerates to create drama. He lies for no particular reason; *pathological liar* comes to my mind.

I cannot begin to untangle any thread of truth from among his lies. His forked-tongue utterances confuse everyone, including himself. How apt Sir Walter Scott's conclusion, "When first we practice to deceive, oh what a tangled web we weave." The snarl of lies is ruining his relationships and reputation.

The only answer I know for this wild child's forked tongue is to focus on one truth, the Lordship of Jesus Christ in his life. My son must surrender control of his tangled web of deceit. He needs to acknowledge his sin and the lack of control that falsehood binds into his life.

The truth of Jesus wins out.

At the name of Jesus every knee should bow, in heaven and on earth and under the earth, and every tongue confess that Jesus Christ is Lord, to the glory of God the Father.
—Philippians 2:10–11

I yearn for my forked-tongued offspring to metamorphose into a man of his word who follows the Truth of the Word.

Whoever of you loves life and desires to see many good days,
keep your tongue from evil and your lips from speaking lies.
Turn from evil and do good; seek peace and pursue it.
—Psalm 34:12–14

*L*ord, enable _____ to love life. Give him/her the desires to see many good days. Teach _____ to keep his/her tongue from evil and his/her lips from speaking lies. Help _____ to turn from evil and do good, to seek peace and pursue it. In Jesus's name. Amen.

◆ ◆ ◆

Petulant Prodigal

*L*ike mother, like daughter. The behaviors I modeled to my daughter are now acted out in her home. Loud, shrill accusations frighten her children. Snide remarks to her husband deflate his male ego.

She tears down her home with rolled eyes followed by words of hurt. The children scurry from her wrath instead of asking her to play. My son-in-law's weary and wary face reveals he expects to be criticized, not appreciated.

My daughter walked away from the Lord in her teenage years. She battles the frustration of being a wife and mother on her own. She does not seek the counsel of the Holy Spirit.

Sadly, she is doing exactly what I did. In my arrogance, I thought I could "do life" on my own. I destroyed my first marriage with insults, sarcasm, and selfishness. I paid a great price by becoming a petulant prodigal. Now I fear my daughter will allow the same mistakes to destroy her home.

I counsel. I pray. I encourage. I hope for the day that my son-in-law and grandchildren will praise her and call her blessed:

Her children arise and call her blessed; her husband also, and he praises her: "Many women do noble things, but you surpass them all."
—Proverbs 31:28–29

Oh Lord, let it be so!

The wise woman builds her house, but with her own hands the foolish one tears hers down.
—Proverbs 14:1

Better to live in a desert than with a quarrelsome and ill-tempered wife.
—Proverbs 21:19

Lord God, help _____ to not be a foolish woman, tearing down her house, but to be wise in building up her home. Let _____ realize it is better for a man to live in the desert than with a quarrelsome and ill-tempered wife. Teach her to be sweet and kind, filled with Your Spirit. In Jesus's name. Amen.

———— ◆ ◆ ◆ ————

Can You Hear Me Now?

The cell phone dropped the call—again. I heard my son swear, redial, and shout, "Can you hear me now? Can you hear me *now*?"

My child's spiritual life resembles the dropped-calls syndrome. Somehow, my son disconnected from God and lost touch with anything that resembles Christianity.

However, God keeps attempting to "dial" back into my son's life. At first, the Lord poured out blessings into my child's life. My child's real estate profession flourished. He stepped up the corporate ladder with ease. Money flowed into his pockets. Unfortunately, my son did not answer God's blessings with a reasonable response; my child instead took the credit for those blessings.

So the Lord took a different tactic to reconnect with my child. C. S. Lewis stated, "God whispers in our pleasures but shouts in our pain." God is now allowing trouble to ring through to my prodigal. My son's prestigious career careens in a downturn. He is close to bankruptcy—the housing market cash cow has dried up. I think God is saying to my son, "Can you hear Me *now*?"

God waits for my son to call 911 collect: "Help! I need You in control of my life."

I pray my son will soon answer God's call. My wild child needs to change his "service" from prideful prodigal to Christ's connection.

I will answer them before they even call to me. While they are still talking to me about their needs, I will go ahead and answer their prayers!
—Isaiah 65:24 (NLT)

*F*ather God, I know that You will answer _____ before he/she even calls to You. I ask that _____ will reconnect with You. While _____ is still talking to You about his/her needs, please go ahead and answer _____'s prayers with intimate conversation with You. In Jesus's name, I pray. Amen.

◆ ◆ ◆

Whispers of Conversations to My Wild Child

Dear Wild Child,

My hairdresser told me today that most of my hair is gray. *Duh!* Every time I glance in the mirror, my hair reflects like a chrome bumper. Moreover, my dear wild child, I believe a few more have sprouted as a result of my concern for you and now my precious grandchildren.

When you were an infant, I read you Bible stories. You heard the stories of the heroes of the faith: Abraham, Moses, Noah, and Deborah—and of course, Jesus the Christ, who changed my life. All through your childhood, I declared God's marvelous deeds. You know the mighty power of the Living God.

Even though you have chosen to walk on a different path of faith, I urge you to allow me to share with your precious little ones the love of God. May I teach them to say their nighttime prayers? Do you care if I share with them how God's mighty deeds changed my life?

My dear child, I love you, but I had no idea how much I would love your children. I swore I would never be an obnoxious, sappy grandma. However, I am. I believe it must have something to do with the shiny chrome-colored hair atop my head.

Thank you for listening to my whispers of conversations. Let me know if I may whisper to my grandchildren too.

Since my youth, O God, you have taught me, and to this day I declare your marvelous deeds. Even when I am old and gray, do not forsake me, O God, till I declare your power to the next generation, your might to all who are to come.
—Psalm 71:17–18

*S*weet Jesus, since my youth You have taught me and to this day I will declare Your marvelous deeds to _____. Even now when I am old and gray, do not forsake my wild child,

_____, or me. Grant us the blessing of declaring Your power to the next generation, the children of _____— my grandchildren. In Your name, I pray. Amen.

❖ ◆ ❖

10

Whispers of Direction

Crossroads

My child stands at several crossroads in life. First, he glances down the road of faith. Next, he stares at the path of peer pressure. Stop and Go flash interchangeably at the intersection of my son's life. Each decision will affect his future.

I realize he must feel torn between two corridors. Like Dorothy in the *Wizard of Oz,* he considers both ways. I attempt to signal yellow cautions in the moments he turns to look at me. I coax. We argue. I post Scripture on the fridge. He shrugs. Scarecrow friends point to an opposite direction.

Today he cares little about the distant mirage of the future. Parental fears engulf my thoughts. I recall, *"Train a child in the way he should go, and when he is old he will not turn from it"* (Proverbs 22:6). I attempt to squelch the worry. The faith-training my child received will not falter.

Suddenly, I comprehend my own crossroads. Will I trust or fear? Trust does not come naturally for me when I lose control of my child's life-changing decisions.

Crossroads create opportunities to trust God. I choose trust.

This is what the LORD says: "Stand at the crossroads and look; ask for the ancient paths, ask where the good way is, and walk in it, and you will find rest for your souls."
—Jeremiah 6:16

*D*ear Father, my child stands at the crossroads of life. I pray for _____to search for the ancient paths of faith. Father, guide _____ _____'s heart to where the good way is and then, keep my child on that path. Father, may _____find rest for his/her soul. In Jesus's name. Amen.

◆ ◆ ◆

Fledgling

The fledgling hummingbird stretched wide its petite dark beak. The mother hovered and then dropped nourishment to the hungry young bird. Satisfied, the fledgling settled back into the mossy gray nest, content to rest in its mother's concerned care.

Nine days later, the same complacent fledgling became an adolescent. It teetered on the nest's edge with wings flapping. The young bird longed to soar beyond safety's boundaries to test its emerging independence. Suddenly, the youngster fell from the nest onto the branch below. Hurriedly, it scooted back to safety, only to begin the stunt all over again.

The fledgling mirrored my son's determined flight from a safe haven, our home: *"A person who strays from home is like a bird that strays from its nest"* (Proverbs 27:8 NLT). He flew from the safe haven of our home into the uncertain wilderness of life.

Now I constantly watch out the window waiting for my son to come home. I observe the fledgling. I study the mother hummingbird. She waits and watches, as I do. Does she hold her breath in fear? No. Mama bird built her nest well. She trusts the fledgling's skillful instincts.

I must trust also. I built our home of faith near the altar of the Cross. My child knows the Way.

Even the sparrow has found a home, and the swallow a nest for herself, where she may have her young— a place near your altar, O LORD Almighty, my King and my God.
—Psalm 84:3

O Lord Almighty, my King, and my God, as my fledgling leaves home to find his/her own nest, I pray _____ discovers a place close to Your altar and to Your heart. Keep _____ safe as he/she strains and struggles to find his/her independence far from my nest. In Jesus's name. Amen.

───────── ♦ ◆ ♦ ─────────

Blind Trust

The German shepherd lay quietly at its master's feet. The brownish muzzle, holding a large tongue, let drool cover the owner's shoes. Oblivious to the dog's slobber, the man reached down and patted the shaggy head. Complete trust emitted from both the dog and owner. They relied on each other.

My eyes lingered on the scene in the coffee shop. Neither blind master nor the guide dog would stumble over obstacles. Their alliance secured protection for each other. I smiled to myself as I noticed doggy shoes shielding even the dog's paw pads from scorching pavement.

My smile turned teary as I thought of my wild child stumbling in a spiritual fog. He needs to trust God. But he refuses to search for the Light—Jesus: *"When Jesus spoke . . . to the people, he said, 'I am the light of the world. Whoever follows me will never walk in darkness, but will have the light of life'"* (John 8:12).

My child trips in this world's darkness and then scrambles back to his feet, only to fall again. His stubborn personality is marred by scrapes with life and resulting cuts and bruises revealed when he interacts with others. Wounded, my child can be irritable and irrational. Sometimes, he reacts in blind rage.

As I leave the coffee shop, I pray that Christ's light will shine in my child's life. I ask that healing cover my child and deliver him from spiritual blindness and its trauma.

And I thank God for the opportunity to witness blind trust. I whisper a prayer for the sightless man and his guide dog with doggy shoes.

"I will lead the blind by ways they have not known, along unfamiliar paths I will guide them; I will turn the darkness into light before them and make the rough places smooth.... I will not forsake them."
—Isaiah 42:16

$\mathcal{D}$ear Lord, lead _____, who is spiritually blind, into a way he/she has not known. Guide _____ to You. Turn _____'s spiritual darkness into light. Lord, I know You will not forsake _____. Protect _____ feet as he/she steps our onto Your path. In Jesus's name. Amen.

◆ ◆ ◆

The Wrong Way

I did not know the old, green pickup truck had that much gumption. It usually stalled more than it rolled forward—however, not tonight. Tonight my son was arrested for drag racing and reckless driving. The highway patrol officer stated that the radar scanned the green machine flying down the road at 90 miles an hour—going the wrong way.

That is the story of my child's life: speeding in the wrong direction. He recklessly abandons every moral value that we teach in our home. My child runs hard and fast from scriptural teaching. He denies that God is.

Nevertheless, my God knows how to turn around a runaway prodigal going the wrong way fast. He has His methods. Jonah's rebellion meant a stormy travail, being tossed into a churning sea, a solitary sojourn, and being vomited onshore. My child's path may include a stay in the county jail for reckless driving in the wrong direction.

But Jonah got up and went in the opposite direction in order to get away from the LORD . . . hoping that by going away to the west he could escape from the LORD.
—Jonah 1:3 (NLT)

He said, "I cried out to the LORD in my great trouble, and he answered me. I called to you from the world of the dead, and LORD, you heard me! . . . " Then the LORD ordered the fish to spit up Jonah on the beach, and it did.
—Jonah 2:2, 10 (NLT)

*D*ear God, _____ goes in the opposite direction in order to get away from You. _____ hopes that he/she can escape You. But God teach _____ to cry out to You. Turn _____ around to the right direction. I pray this in the name of Jesus. Amen.

—————— ◆ ◆ ◆ ——————

Dribbles and Dabbles

*K*eep your children busy! Sports are a great outlet for pent-up energy. Athletics keeps kids out of trouble."

127

Uhh…not so much always!

I watch my son dribble the basketball up and down the shiny wood court. He is adept at maneuvering the ball away from his opponent—almost as good as he is at outwitting me with his devious movements. My son usually wins both games.

He dribbles the ball; he dabbles in drugs. He shouts at the coach; he defies his mother. He sprints the court; he drinks beer. He throws the ball; he heaves his guts.

I seek wisdom in how to raise my son. I ask for wisdom as Solomon did: *"Give me wisdom and knowledge, that I may guide this child, for who is able to direct him?"* (personal application of 2 Chronicles 1:10).

I continue to watch as my son blocks, tips, and shoots the basketball. His robust frame displays determination. His athletic skill intimidates his opponents. (He intimidates me too.) He dribbles past me without a glance. Up he leaps; he shoots and scores. His team wins. He is the hero, again.

Uhh…not so much!

Now comes the after-game party. He will dabble in things he should not. My son will drag home, depleted of energy. I will find evidence that after the game, he was not a hero, but a hoodlum.

Please Lord God, I need a dribble of wisdom and a dabble of parenting skills right this moment!

Say a quiet yes to God and he'll be there in no time. Quit dabbling in sin. Purify your inner life. Quit playing the field.
—James 4:8 (*The Message*)

*D*ear Lord, help _____ to say a quiet yes to You. I know You will answer _____ immediately. Teach _____ to quit dabbling in sin. Help _____ to purify his/her inner life and quit playing on the court of sin. In Jesus's name. Amen.

What a Drag!

Ireceived a call from a hospital today. The nurse sounded slightly annoyed as she said, "Your son's been in an accident. Can you come down immediately?"

"Of course, I am on my way," I said. "Is he all right?" I asked, but the curt nurse had already hung up the phone.

I raced to the hospital with my heart thudding in my ears. Prayers slipped from my lips as I screeched around every turn. "Oh, God, please let my son be all right."

The sliding glass doors slid open and I sprinted into the emergency room. I was escorted back behind a covered curtain where my son lay with a scraped and bruised face. Immediately, I knew he was going to be fine, but wondered what happened to damage his face.

Come to find out, he had been auto surfing behind a pickup truck. My son stood on his skateboard and held onto the tailgate, and off they went. They had a great time, until he lost his grip and planted himself face-first into the asphalt.

Now instead of fear, fury arose in my mother's heart. "What were you thinking?" I asked.

"I dunno. Brandon did it first, and then I did. I think I must have hit a rock or something. Mom, do you know if they picked up my skateboard?"

I thought my child knew better than to do something so stupid. I lectured him that he could have been killed, blah, blah, blah... I saw his eyes begin to glaze over, not from the pain medication, but from my harangue.

"Well son, it's a drag, literally. And no, I think your board is gone for good."

And I promise to obey! With all my heart I want your blessings. Be merciful just as you promised. I thought about the wrong direction in which I was headed, and turned around and came

running back to you. Evil men have tried to drag me into sin,
but I am firmly anchored to your laws.
—Psalm 119:57–61 (TLB)

*F*ather, teach _____ to obey You. Let _____
want Your blessings with all his/her heart. Be merciful to
_____, as You promised. Aid _____
in recognizing the wrong direction in which he/she is headed. Turn
_____ around. Evil people have tried to drag _____
into sin, but I ask that _____ be firmly anchored to Your
laws. In Jesus's name. Amen.

———————— ◆ ◆ ◆ ————————

The Quiet One

The headlines pronounced another shooting at a school. Several
students were injured in the fray. The investigators believe it was a
fellow student—the one nicknamed "The Quiet One."

My child is quiet. He sits by himself, lost in deep thoughts;
impenetrable by others. He refuses to discuss anything other than the
mundane happenings of life: the weather, what's for dinner, and who
won the Monday Night Football game are allowable subject matter.
But no one dares to go beyond into his personal territory. The fury in
his eyes terrifies me.

Counselors and therapists say not to worry. "He'll grow out of it.
Young adulthood is difficult." But I perceive something more sinister
than life transition in his brooding thoughts.

"Are not my few days almost over? Turn away from me so
I can have a moment's joy before I go to the place of no return,
to the land of gloom and deep shadow, to the land of deepest

night, of deep shadow and disorder, where even the light is like darkness."
—Job 10:20–22

I have nowhere else to turn than to my Jesus. He knows my child's deepest, darkest thoughts. So I place my quiet one into His nail-scarred hands and whisper prayers of directions. Then, I wait quietly.

I am still confident of this: I will see the goodness of the LORD in the land of the living. Wait for the LORD; be strong and take heart and wait for the LORD.
—Psalm 27:13–14

$\mathcal{L}$ord, I am confident that I will see Your goodness in _____. Show _____ the land of the living. Remove from _____ the brooding gloom that steeps inside. Teach _____ and me to wait for You. Help us to be strong and to take heart. In Jesus's name. Amen.

——————— ◆ ◆ ◆ ———————

Missed Flight

$\mathbf{S}$he spent the night in the Miami airport. She put on her headphones, laid her head on the dirty carpet, and slept until morning. She missed her flight because she goofed around packing her canvas backpack. "Do I have my music? Where's a plastic bag for my wet bikini?"

She chatted with a friend on her cell phone instead of checking in at the gate. The plane took off, minus my lackadaisical daughter.

I am concerned that if the Lord returns to catch His children up in the air, my daughter will miss that flight too. The most important flight in all eternity could be without my beloved child.

Faith holds no interest for her. She prefers New Age–type philosophy. It is all about crystals and freedom of thought. A belief system with no structure attracts my free-spirited offspring. She insists, "Life's ebb and flow will direct my spirit."

I want to yell, "You can't even make a flight from Miami with a paper ticket in your hand. How are 'life's ebb and flow' going to direct you?" However, that approach will not work; but prayer will. Prayer is *the* ticket, because I personally know the Pilot of the direct flight to heaven. Moreover, He does not want anyone to miss His flight.

After that, we who are still alive and are left will be caught up together with them in the clouds to meet the Lord in the air. And so we will be with the Lord forever.
—1 Thessalonians 4:17

*P*recious Jesus, reveal to _____ that You will be coming back for Your children. Allow _____ to accept the truth that those who are alive will be caught up in the clouds to meet You in the air. Lord Jesus, I ask that_____ will be with You forever. In Your name. Amen.

◆ ◆ ◆

Roadrunner

*B*eep! Beep! My son reminds me of the crazed wild-haired roadrunner. He runs back and forth, leaving nothing but dust and stopping for only a moment to "Beep! Beep!" a comment or two. He never slows down, but runs in crisscross patterns with no sure direction in his life. His enemy conceals himself out of sight to bring catastrophe and defeat.

Sadly, Satan is hiding in wait for my child. In a frenzy, my son's behavior is oblivious to the real danger. This life is not an imaginary game. The Bible advises, *"Put on the whole armor of God, that you may be able to stand against the wiles of the devil"* (Ephesians 6:11 NKJV). My son puts on no spiritual armor for himself. It is only by God's grace and a mother's prayer that my child has not been demolished by the wiles of devil.

It may take a stumble and fall to slow down this child who runs with reckless abandon. Alternatively, it may take a bonk on the head by the devil to bring my scatterbrained son to his senses. Or possibly, it may take the hand of God putting a divine stop sign in the path of my child to bring direction to his life and peace to my heart.

> *This is what the LORD says— your Redeemer, the Holy One of Israel: "I am the LORD your God, who teaches you what is best for you, who directs you in the way you should go. If only you had paid attention to my commands, your peace would have been like a river, your righteousness like the waves of the sea."*
> —Isaiah 48:17–18

*F*ather, You are the Lord God. Teach _____ what is best for him/her. Direct _____ in the way he/she should go. Instruct _____ to pay attention to Your commands, so that _____'s peace will be like a river and his/her righteousness like the waves of the sea. In Jesus's name. Amen.

——————— ◆ ◆ ◆ ———————

Whispers of Direction to My Wild Child

Dear Wild Child,

Your face displays confusion and torment. I watch you wrestle with each decision. You pace the floors. Bitten fingernails and cuticles

133

give away your anxiety concerning what direction to take in so many areas of your life.

Try to recall from your Sunday School years the picture of the Good Shepherd standing beside a flock of peaceful sheep. Do you remember the one sheep straying off into the distance? Its wooly head cocked, looking back at the Shepherd to see if He noticed the errant behavior.

Well, my wild child, you remind me of that little straying sheep. You know where peace and tranquility can be found—next to the Shepherd. However, you insist on taking your own direction—a route that lacks peace and confidence. I know you realize that danger lurks around the corners of your wild living, but still you stray further into uncharted territory.

Child, come back under the Shepherd's watch. He will protect you. He will give you direction in your life. You will find peace of mind when you submit to His tender care. I am praying the Shepherd's crook wraps around your heart. He is able to restore your soul...and your fingernails, dear child.

He makes me lie down in green pastures, he leads me beside quiet waters, he restores my soul. He guides me in paths of righteousness for his name's sake.
—Psalm 23:2–3

𝓛ord Jesus, make _____ lie down in the safety of Your green pastures of love. Lead _____ beside quiet waters. Restore _____'s soul. Guide _____ in paths of righteousness for Your name's sake. I pray this in Your name. Amen.

◆ ◆ ◆

11

Whispers of Patience

No Limit

The worst of sinners—that was me. I understood the Lord's unlimited patience. I saw His great mercy. I knew God. I loved Him. Yet I walked away in impatience and anger at His will for my life.

Now I watch my daughter do exactly the same thing. She knows Christ Jesus. She loves Him. Now her anger and lack of understanding drive her away from God. My daughter bellows belligerent accusations at God. "Why did this happen? What type of God would allow this in *my* life?" She barrels into rebellious behavior while shaking her fist at God. "I'll show You who is in charge of my life!" state her defiant actions.

Thankfully, my mother prayed with patience for her wild child, and I will pray with mercy for my prodigal daughter. Because I lived as a prodigal for several years, I understand God's unlimited patience with a resentful rebel.

Jesus is able to woo her back with love. His compassion is able to soften her resentment. God's tenderness is able to lure my daughter back into His arms. The patience of God is able to win out over the confusion that filters through her thoughts.

She can return to God because His mercy and compassion hold no limits.

But for that very reason I was shown mercy so that in me, the worst of sinners, Christ Jesus might display his unlimited patience as an example for those who would believe on him and receive eternal life.
—1 Timothy 1:16

*D*ear Heavenly Father, I pray for You to show mercy to _____, a sinner, so that Christ Jesus might display His unlimited patience. Use me as an example for encouraging _____ to believe in Jesus and receive eternal life. Then let _____'s life be an example of Your unlimited mercy and patience too. In Jesus's name. Amen.

◆ ◆ ◆

Pill of Ill Will

*S*he plots. She plans. She executes her mean-spiritedness with precision. She is a pain in the neck. She is a pill of ill will. She is my daughter.

Always a difficult child, my daughter has become intolerable. She insists on being the center of attention—one way or the other. Usually she opts for *the other*. For example, on the way to her sister's wedding, she became infuriated with me over a trivial matter. My little pill jumped out of the moving car and slid across the pavement. The matrimonial ceremony stalled as the wedding party headed for the emergency room with her howling in pain.

Or what about the time I answered a knock at the door to my consternation? There stood two primly clothed, stern-faced women. "We're from the Child Welfare Agency. Your daughter reports that you have been abusing her."

"What?"

I invited them in and explained that I had taken her cell phone away as a disciplinary measure. "Does that constitute child abuse? I don't think so!"

Nonplussed, they agreed with me. "However, we still need to file a report," they apologized.

My daughter peeped over the banister as the door closed. She smirked. She skipped back to her room.

That's my daughter. I love her, but she is a tough pill to swallow!

For this very reason, make every effort to add to your faith goodness; and to goodness, knowledge; and to knowledge, self-control; and to self-control, perseverance; and to perseverance, godliness; and to godliness, brotherly kindness; and to brotherly kindness, love.
—2 Peter 1:5–7

*F*ather, I pray for _____; please rework his/her disposition. Teach_____ to have faith in You. Then I pray that _____ will gravitate toward goodness, knowledge, and self-control. I ask You to initiate in _____ the character traits of perseverance, godliness, and, most of all, kindness. Teach _____ kindness! In Jesus's name. Amen.

——————— ◆ ◆ ◆ ———————

Birth Pains

I pushed to no avail. After 48 hours of hard labor, my son was not coming out anytime soon. Stubborn—he was, from birth. Eventually, both the doctor and I gave in. We opted for a caesarean delivery. The recovery was painful, but the baby was born.

My child is still stubborn. He refuses to go to church. He doubts that the kingdoms of God and hell even exist. His obstinacy conflicts with everything he has been taught in our home. My child is not a follower of Christ Jesus.

So I am in "labor" again, but this time, it is with spiritual birth pains for my child. This birth process creates a deep anguish in my soul. I push in prayer. If only I could have a heavenly epidural while I implore the Spirit to bring forth new life in my son.

However, I will labor on in spiritual birth pains for my child. If it takes 48 hours or 48 years, I will keep praying for my child's spiritual rebirth.

I will stay in the divine delivery room until my child is in the kingdom of God. My child will be born of the flesh and of the Spirit.

Jesus answered, "I tell you the truth, no one can enter the kingdom of God unless he is born of water and the Spirit. Flesh gives birth to flesh, but the Spirit gives birth to spirit. You should not be surprised at my saying, 'You must be born again.'"
—John 3:5–7

*L*ord Jesus, allow _____ to see the truth that no one will be in the kingdom of God unless he/she is born again. I pray for my child, _____, to be born again, of Your Spirit. In Your name, I pray. Amen.

◆ ◆ ◆

Raw Clay

One description of my child would be this: willful and wayward. My child's life runs amok because she refuses to kowtow for anyone or anything, including God.

My child revolts against anything that hints of tradition. Her outward appearance draws stares from onlookers. A tongue stud, purple hair, baggy black clothes, and gothic makeup disguise her innate cuteness. My child glares, as if daring someone to comment on her anarchist style.

Unfortunately, the willfulness and waywardness worms its way out from the inside. Dark scowls replace the grins that used to frame her face. Harsh words pour out from the silver-studded tongue, where once girlish giggles emerged. Inner turmoil seethes in my child's soul.

Frustration with life floods her young adult world. Because she is strong willed, she wants to be in control, to make her own decisions. However, life does not allow it. Various circumstances thwart her efforts to be the boss of life. She is furious at not being in control. So she acts out her anger as a wild child.

I watch her with patience. Time and maturity will mold her. God is still the potter, and He is still working in her life. She is a piece of work all right, but not a finished piece. She is still raw clay.

Yet, O LORD, you are our Father. We are the clay, you are the potter; we are all the work of your hand. Do not be angry beyond measure, O LORD; do not remember our sins forever. Oh, look upon us, we pray, for we are all your people.
—Isaiah 64:8–9

*O*h Lord, You are Father. _____ is the clay. You are the potter. We are all the work of Your hand. Do not be angry beyond measure, Oh Lord with my child, _____. Do not remember the sins of _____ forever. Oh, look upon _____, I pray, for she is Your creation. In Jesus's name. Amen.

"Punk Kid"

My father would roll over in his grave if he could see his grandchild now. I know exactly what he would say: "That punk kid! He has everything in life and just look at him! Ingrate! What a punk!"

The term *punk* was the most derogatory term my dad could think of to say. The word meant worthless, inadequate, and a poor example of a human being.

Now that does not describe my child correctly. My child is a great human being. He is not worthless or inadequate. However, my child is bratty. Sometimes he *acts* like a punk, according to my father's definition.

It is funny how words and definitions change over time. My son calls himself a "punk rocker." He wears his punk clothing. Punk music blares from his guitar. He is a punk and proud of it!

As the mother of this punk rocker, I can see both sides to *punk*. He *is* ungrateful. He shuns acknowledging his Christian faith with his friends. He likes to show off and be mouthy to me in front of his buddies. He is talented musically. He wears bizarre clothing that will eventually wind up in the donation box. Yes, for now my child is a punk by both definitions.

Thankfully, my daddy does not see this punk. Moreover, I have to admit that when my child walks away from me with a snotty attitude, I think to myself, *Punk kid!* Nevertheless, my goal as this "punk's" mother is to love and encourage him until he outgrows this phase. I hope it is soon.

My goal is that they will be encouraged and knit together by strong ties of love. I want them to have full confidence because they have complete understanding of God's secret plan, which is Christ himself.
—Colossians 2:2 (NLT)

$\mathcal{F}$ather, my goal is that _____ will be encouraged and knit into a grateful Christian by strong ties of love. I ask for _____ to have full confidence in You, with complete understanding of Your secret plan, Christ Himself. In Jesus's name. Amen.

◆ ◆ ◆

Get Over It!

I want to scream, "Get over it!" I am tired of trying to convince my child to let go of past hurts. Yes, her parents divorced. Yes, we lived on welfare for a time. Yes, life is not fair. Even Jesus told us that life is hard: *"I have told you these things, so that in me you may have peace. In this world you will have trouble. But take heart! I have overcome the world"* (John 16:33).

My child holds on to bitterness and anger like a stuffed toy. As though it comforts her. She does not want to let it go. She excuses the malice that rises up in her by tying it to her pitiful past. "It's not my fault. If my childhood would have been different, then I wouldn't act this way."

"Yeah, right," I mutter under my breath.

A line from the *Phantom of the Opera* reverberates in my head: "You try my patience!" My daughter tries my patience. It is becoming more difficult for me not to lash back at her with words of harsh contempt for her bratty bitterness.

Once again, I seek the solace of the Holy Spirit. "Infuse me with Your patience. Please counsel me with Your wisdom in how to handle my child's bitterness. And help us *both* to get over it!"

Get rid of all bitterness, rage and anger, brawling and slander, along with every form of malice. Be kind and compassionate to one another, forgiving each other, just as in Christ God

141

forgave you.
—Ephesians 4:31–32

*F*ather, help _____ to get rid of all bitterness, rage, and anger. Renew _____'s soul so that he/she does not act in malice. In addition, Lord, help me to be kind and compassionate with _____. Help us both to forgive each other as You forgave us. In Jesus's name. Amen.

——————— ◆ ◆ ◆ ———————

In Time

And provide for those who grieve in Zion, to bestow on them a crown of beauty instead of ashes, the oil of gladness instead of mourning, and a garment of praise instead of a spirit of despair. They will be called oaks of righteousness, a planting of the LORD for the display of his splendor.
—Isaiah 61:3

I grieve with bitter tears for my daughter. Her life has evolved so differently than I expected. I recall the comments from family, friends, and teachers during her elementary years: "She is so energetic." "Your daughter possesses leadership skills." "The sky is the limit for a girl with her potential."

But somewhere between childhood and adulthood, my girl changed. She became somber. A reserve crept into her personality. I remember, one day, watching her in my car's rearview mirror. She sat quietly with her head turned to look out the window. Her rambunctious brothers teased her, but she refused to acknowledge the pests. I thought, *Something has changed.*

In hindsight, I wondered if some type of sexual abuse had taken place, but when questioned in that direction, she denied it.

Yet *something* happened. She went from extrovert to introvert. My daughter went from highly driven to minimal effort. She traveled a path from gladness to despair.

I grieve for my daughter and her despondency. But I claim 2 Timothy 1:12: *"For I know whom I have believed, and am persuaded that he is able to keep that which I have committed unto him against that day"* (KJV). In time, perhaps not until heaven, my daughter will be restored to a display of His splendor.

*D*ear Lord, please provide for _____, who seems to be grieving. Help me to help_____ overcome what he/she faces. And bestow on _____ a crown of beauty instead of ashes, the oil of gladness instead of mourning, and a garment of praise instead of a spirit of despair. Reveal to _____ that he/she will be called an oak of righteousness, a planting of the Lord for the display of Your splendor. In Jesus's name. Amen.

Courageous Discouragement

Discouragement darts into our lives like a quick-moving hummingbird. My wild child and I feel that things are finally improving, when suddenly my child messes up his life again. We skip one step forward and stumble three steps backward.

My patience wears thin. My anger flares up in the moment of frustration. Fear for my child's future stalks my nights. I cling to God's Word to keep my courage from turning into complete discouragement.

I vow to hold tightly to the promises for my child's future. Courage and strength will flow from the hand of God into our lives. It will be through His encouragement that we will survive the seemingly endless battle of poor choices my wild child makes.

I whisper to God, "Lord, stay by my side as Your courage battles my discouragement."

"Study this Book of the Law continually. Meditate on it day and night so you may be sure to obey all that is written in it. Only then will you succeed. I command you—be strong and courageous! Do not be afraid or discouraged. For the LORD your God is with you wherever you go."
—Joshua 1:8–9 (NLT)

*L*ord God, teach _____ to study Your Word continually. Instruct _____ in how to meditate on it day and night so that he/she may be sure to obey all that is written in it. Only then will _____ succeed. You command us to be strong and courageous. Help _____ and myself not to be afraid or discouraged. For You, the Lord our God, is with us wherever we go. In Jesus's name. Amen.

◆ ◆ ◆

Espresso Exasperation

The frothy espresso's heat stung my hand as I carried the double-cupped drink to my table. At the same time, anger steamed in my thoughts. *How dare she do this to me again! That's it; I am tired of all her self-seeking rudeness.*

The coffee spilled over onto my hand as I walked. A scarlet mark instantly appeared. It hurt. Tears sprang to my eyes from the pain on my hand, but more so from the ache in my heart.

Exasperation at my daughter consumed me. At my wit's end, I had left our house after another screaming argument with her. I could not stand to be around her another moment. As I slammed the front door, the thought was there: *I hate her.*

However, now as my coffee cooled, so did my fury. I glanced down at the crimson burn on my hand—a record left by the espresso but also our disagreement. I thought back to the cutting remarks I made to my daughter during our battle. I had shouted out a record of all her past mistakes.

My rudeness prevailed. Kindness disappeared. My love for my daughter evaporated into exasperation.

I left the coffee shop with my espresso and a newly purchased one for my daughter. I would not allow pride to keep me from apologizing.

"The end of a matter is better than its beginning, and patience is better than pride" (Ecclesiastes 7:8). The end of this argument will be better than the beginning. I will not allow my pride to override my patience for my child.

Love is patient, love is kind. It does not envy, it does not boast, it is not proud. It is not rude, it is not self-seeking, it is not easily angered, it keeps no record of wrongs.
—1 Corinthians 13:4–5

*S*weet Jesus, let me show Your patience and kindness to _____. Help me not to be rude to my child, _____. Help me not to be easily angered with _____ _____. Most importantly, let me keep no record of the wrongs of _____. In Your name, I pray. Amen.

◆ ◆ ◆

Whispers of Patience to My Wild Child

Dear Wild Child,

I watched as you ping-ponged around the room. You opened drawers, rolled a chair across the floor, tore the white paper on the

145

exam table, and yanked the blinds up and down. I already knew what the diagnosis would be.

Just then, the pediatrician strode into the room. He announced the verdict: "Your child has attention deficit hyperactivity disorder, more commonly known as ADHD."

I looked around at the shambles of his examination room and wanted to say, "Really?"

I once heard the advice, "Don't pray for patience, because God will allow things in your life to produce patience." Maybe I prayed for patience before you were born—I don't know.

As you know, dear child, patience is not my strongest suit when it comes to personality traits. You now try my patience with your spirited rebellion. I admit that your defiance of my parental authority makes me angry and that I want to retaliate against you.

However, I want you to know that even though I lose my patience with you, I *do* love you. And I need you to know that God *loves* you and He is patient. He created you just the way you are—ADHD and all.

So, my child, go ahead—yank open the blinds to heaven and roll into the arms of God. He is waiting patiently for you.

The Lord is not slow in keeping his promise, as some understand slowness. He is patient with you, not wanting anyone to perish, but everyone to come to repentance.
—2 Peter 3:9

*O*h Lord, thank You for Your patience with _____. Reveal to _____ that You are not slow in keeping Your promises, but that You are being patient with him/her, not wanting anyone to perish. Bring my child, _____, to repentance. In Jesus's name. Amen.

◆ ◆ ◆

12

Whispers of Trust

Party Time

My child sneaks contraband into her room. A pill will occasionally roll out from all the clutter on the floor. I believe my daughter barters and sells a variety of ill-gotten prescription drugs to her friends. Then when the weekend rolls around, it is party time for her. Prescription drug use abounds at "pharm parties"—replacing beer and marijuana use.

However, when I confront her, she swears she would never do such a thing.

"Mom, I am not dropping drugs! All I ever take is an aspirin when I am on my period. You simply don't trust me!"

She is right. I do not trust her. Deep inside my gut, I know she is lying to me. I have experienced her altered moods. (And it is not PMS.) She does not act sloppy stoned, but ethereal. Dilated eyes and the lazy smile tip me off that she is a little "happier" than normal. It is "party time" in my wild child's young body and mind.

Last week the school sent home a newsletter, relaying information on the rampant prescription drug misuse in the high schools. They asked us to lock up any type of drugs that may be available for the teens to snatch out of the medicine cabinet.

My child is not getting them from home, but she is getting them from someone. Moreover, I think she is supplying the "happy pills" to her friends. We are going to start a weekly drug test in our home. If she passes, great! However, if she fails, that will end her party time.

The LORD is my strength and my shield; my heart trusts in him, and I am helped. My heart leaps for joy and I will give thanks to him in song.
—Psalm 28:7

*D*ear Lord, be the strength and shield for _____. Help him/her not to depend on prescription drugs for happiness. My heart trusts in You. Show _____ Your trustworthiness. Let _____'s heart leap for joy because of You. And I will give thanks to You forever. In Jesus's name. Amen.

◆ ◆ ◆

Missing Piece

*S*he lost the retainer... again.

"Lord, I can't afford another retainer. Please let me find it," I prayed.

She "misplaced" her retainer while partying at the park. I scrambled through the park's soft grass and sand searching for the missing mouthpiece. Furious at my daughter for not caring enough to take responsibility for what I worked so hard to provide, I searched frantically. At 17, she knew better. I alternated between complaining and praying.

Her party lifestyle cost the family not only in monetary value but also in the disruption of our relationship. I felt the strain of both. I stopped searching as I began to cry. I wept for my daughter. I wept for myself. My daughter was as lost as her dental hardware.

A warm breeze dried my tears. A gentle reassurance poured into my heart. I realized God had not misplaced my daughter. He never loses track of her whereabouts (or her retainer's either).

As I pushed myself up, I felt a sharp edge of plastic protruding from the grass. I pulled and suddenly a small piece of the missing retainer lay in my hand—broken. I smiled up at the sky. I clipped my key chain to the silver-wire band that remained attached to the hot pink plastic. A memento to remind me that although my daughter might be broken, the Shepherd has not misplaced her.

"I will place shepherds over them who will tend them, and they will no longer be afraid or terrified, nor will any be missing," *declares the* LORD.
—Jeremiah 23:4

*L*ord, shepherd _____. Calm my own heart so I am no longer afraid or terrified. Help me to realize _____ is not missing in Your sight. In Jesus's name. Amen.

———————— ◆ ◆ ◆ ————————

Cinderella Syndrome

The Cinderella syndrome struck our home again today. My long and lanky stepdaughter lashed out at me. She loomed over me and shouted her disgruntlement at me. Then with a closing obscenity, she screamed, "You're not my mother!"

She swears I dislike her and that I treat her unfairly. That is not true. I love her and want to be a friend, not her mother. I am afraid she will never like me because her dad married me. The marriage shattered the fantasy that her mother and dad would reunite someday.

This crumpled dream expresses itself in disappointment and bitterness. She rejects my overtures of friendship. It enrages her that I will not

149

cower when she towers over me. She intends to make my life miserable. (She is trying to do a fine job!) However, I will not give up hope.

She is my husband's daughter—my daughter. She is a trust given to me for the rest of my life. I will remain faithful to the trust. I recite, *"The LORD himself goes before you and will be with you; he will never leave you nor forsake you. Do not be afraid; do not be discouraged"* (Deuteronomy 31:8).

So I will not fear or be discouraged. I will love her as a mom loves. I will treat her as a friend. She is a God-given trust. I pray that my daughter, regardless of how she now rebels, will embrace life as a child of God.

My Cinderella may feel wretched and unloved, but she is a princess to me.

Now it is required that those who have been given a trust must prove faithful.
—1 Corinthians 4:2

$\mathcal{D}$ear Father God, I know I have been given a trust in regard to _____ as my stepchild. Help me to prove faithful in Your and _____'s sight. In Jesus's name, I pray. Amen.

———————— ◆ ◆ ◆ ————————

Abandoned

For the LORD your God is a merciful God; he will not abandon or destroy you.
—Deuteronomy 4:31

$\mathbf{M}$y child trusts no one. The distrust results from abandonment. Trust departed the day his father walked out of our lives. Suspicion moved in; it tried to shove God out.

How can a child be taught to trust an unseen God? Who can teach a fatherless child to pray, *"Our Father in heaven, may your name be honored"* (Matthew 6:9 NLT)?

Why would a deserted child believe the following words of Jesus?

> *"And so I tell you, keep on asking, and you will be given what you ask for. Keep on looking, and you will find. Keep on knocking, and the door will be opened. For everyone who asks, receives. Everyone who seeks, finds. And the door is opened to everyone who knocks.*
>
> *"You fathers—if your children ask for a fish, do you give them a snake instead? Or if they ask for an egg, do you give them a scorpion? Of course not!"*
> —Luke 11:9–12 (NLT)

Trust does not come easily for anyone. Trust evaporates instantly in the child abandoned by a parent. Instead, a hard shell of defense and independence emerges as a shield against the possibility of more personal rejection.

But the Father God *never* abandons His children. No matter how they act or what they may say, He still loves unconditionally. *"His faithful love endures forever!"* (1 Chronicles 16:34 NLT).

My child may have abandoned the hope of a loving *human* father, and therefore the belief in God the Father. However, that does not distort the truth—my child's heavenly Father waits for the wild child to return to faith in Him.

$\mathcal{L}$ord God, You are merciful. Show Your mercy to my child, _____. You are a heavenly Father, able to assure _____ that You will never abandon him/her. In Jesus's name, I pray. Amen.

◆ ◆ ◆

Mutual Distrust

*To discipline and reprimand a child produces wisdom, but a
mother is disgraced by an undisciplined child.*
—Proverbs 29:15 (NLT)

Mark Twain pegged human nature in *Tom Sawyer*. The young rogue,
Tom, believed that Aunt Polly was too strict and did not understand
a boy's needs. Aunt Polly loved Tom, but never trusted him completely.
In fact, they held a mutual distrust of each other.

My child and I live out a relationship like that of Aunt Polly and
young Tom. My child rebels against anything I ask, though I always
have his best interests at heart. In response, I watch his wild antics,
and I *am* ready to disapprove at the slightest hint of misbehavior. The
mutual distrust hinders our love for each other.

I want to be a good mom, but my Tom Sawyer makes it difficult to
see beyond the day-to-day discipline. The constant monitoring wears me
out. (And I am positive he is annoyed too.) What is a mother to do?

The story of Tom and Aunt Polly ended on a happy note. They both
realized that they loved and cared for each other. Tom probably still
found himself in trouble. (On the other hand, trouble found him because
that was the nature of his character.) Moreover, in all likelihood, Aunt
Polly probably still smothered him with a watchful eye.

I want that ending too. A mother's heart will not change and a child's
antics will not soon dissipate. However, an overprotective mom and her
wild child can learn to trust the *love* they have for each other.

Dear Lord, teach me how to discipline and reprimand _____ in a
way that will produce wisdom in _____. I pray that somehow we
both learn how to overcome our mistrust of each other. Allow _____
to understand my love and concern. In Your name, I pray. Amen.

❖ ◆ ❖

Bargain Hunter

My wild child can sniff out the potential for a haggling session, and his adrenaline begins to skyrocket. He *loves* to bargain.

Unfortunately, he also barters with God. My son sins with enthusiasm. Then he plots how to blot out the sin with good behaviors. He approaches God with the attitude of, "Hey God, let's bargain Saturday's sin against Sunday's self-sacrifice." He wants to do life on his own terms, but, at the same time, he wants God's approval.

The problem is, my son does not entirely trust God's forgiveness. He thinks, *How can it be so easy to just ask forgiveness? There needs to be some sort of wheeling and dealing.*

My wild child is up against the Ultimate Bargain Provider. The Lord God answers back to my child's train of thought with words from Isaiah: "'*Come now, let us argue this out,' says the* LORD. *'No matter how deep the stain of your sins, I can remove it. I can make you as clean as freshly fallen snow. Even if you are stained as red as crimson, I can make you as white as wool'*" (Isaiah 1:18 NLT).

Thankfully, I am caught between the two—my son, the hunter, and my God, the Provider. I stand as witness to them both. I will pray for my son to trust Jesus Christ as his Savior. I will ask that the Holy Spirit keep on reasoning with my wild child until he accepts the grace of God—freely given.

> *"Don't bargain with God. Be direct. Ask for what you need. This isn't a cat-and-mouse, hide-and-seek game we're in."*
> —Matthew 7:7–8 (*The Message*)

Lord Jesus, train _____ to ask You for what he/she needs. Let him/her realize a relationship with You is not a game to love; it is Love. I ask this in Your name, Jesus. Amen.

◆ ◆ ◆

Hitchhiker

My wild child was hitchhiking at night! This son of mine, with torn jeans, hair tied in a ponytail, and a guitar slung over his shoulders, wanders the highways with his thumb out. It was darling when, as a toddler, he sucked his thumb and then pointed it to what he wanted on the shelf. It is not cute anymore. It frightens me to think of what could happen to this young man as he hitchhikes across the country.

If only I could still place my son in time-out. I would sit him in the corner for an hour or more (probably a lot more). However, he now is of age and no longer underneath my maternal jurisdiction for punishment.

"Ah, it's OK, Mom. Nothin's gonna happen to me. Where's your trust?"

Where is my trust? I ask myself.

I respond, "I trust God. I do *not* trust the crazy world we live in. Hitchhiking is not a safe mode of travel." Then I quote, *"Wise people think before they act; fools don't and even brag about it"*!

"Whatever," he counters. He strolls out the door chewing on a guitar pick. The conversation ends.

Oh, but my conversation with God is only beginning. My child needs to learn to trust God, not his own errant decisions. I may not have maternal jurisdiction anymore, but I can snitch on my wild child to the Father.

Who among you fears the LORD and obeys the word of his servant? Let him who walks in the dark, who has no light, trust in the name of the LORD and rely on his God.
—Isaiah 50:10

Father God, teach _____ to revere You. Help _____ to obey Your Word. Let _____ not walk

in the darkness any longer. Teach _____ to trust in Your
name and to rely on You as his/her God. In Jesus's name. Amen.

◆ ◆ ◆

Tripped Up

*K*aboom! Once again, my child falls into temptation. My daughter
repeatedly trips on the same sin. Raised in the faith, she knows
better; yet she blames God for her mistakes.

"It's not my fault. God places the temptation right there in front of
me," she says.

I respond, "No, that's not it. Scripture tells us, *'When tempted, no
one should say, "God is tempting me." For God cannot be tempted by
evil, nor does he tempt anyone'"* (James 1:13).

"But, I can't stand it. It's just too tempting for me to say no," she
says in rebuttal.

*"'No test or temptation that comes your way is beyond the course
of what others have had to face. All you need to remember is that God
will never let you down; he'll never let you be pushed past your limit;
he'll always be there to help you come through it.'* (1 Corinthians 10:13
The Message)," I counter.

She cries.

I wrap my arms around her shaking shoulders. "Honey, let's pray.
God wants you to put your trust in Him when temptation comes. He
will help you. Let's pray that you won't be tripped up again by this
same old sin."

She nods her head without looking up at me.

We begin praying the Lord's model prayer:

*"'Our Father in heaven, hallowed be your name, your kingdom
come, your will be done on earth as it is in heaven. Give us
today our daily bread. Forgive us our debts, as we also have*

155

forgiven our debtors. And lead us not into temptation, but deliver us from the evil one.'"
—Matthew 6:9–13

*The L*ORD* is good, a refuge in times of trouble. He cares for those who trust in him.*
—Nahum 1:7

*L*ord God, reveal to _____ Your goodness. Allow my child to recognize that You are a refuge in times of trouble. Show _____ that You care for those who trust in You. In Jesus's name. Amen.

———————— ◆ ◆ ◆ ————————

Checkmate

*M*y child knows the Lord. He will go to church, but finds it somewhat boring. He will sing the praise songs. My son will even read his Bible occasionally. However, he has not discovered an *intimate* relationship with God on a daily basis.

My son tends to stray to the wild side of life. He toys with temptation. He flirts with lady luck. He sticks his toes into the tip of temptation and then pulls out before the quicksand of sin sucks him in. Nevertheless, one of these days, he may step too far in, and the devil will yank hard and fast. Satan lies in wait for my child. The Scripture warns us about such: *"Be careful! Watch out for attacks from the Devil, your great enemy. He prowls around like a roaring lion, looking for some victim to devour"* (1 Peter 5:8 NLT).

I stress to my child the importance of a daily relationship with Christ. I buy him devotional books. I offer to send him on mission trips. I hang Scriptures on the fridge that he frequents every hour.

However, for every godly maneuver I take, Satan contrives a countermove. The bombardment of evil enticement escalates. It is tit for tat. However, I know how to thwart the evil one in his game for my son's faith.

I pray according to God's Word! I ask for my child's protection from the evil one. My God will protect and strengthen my child's faith—for my God is faithful and will accomplish His purposes.

My prayer is not that you take them out of the world but that you protect them from the evil one.
—John 17:15

The Lord is faithful, and he will strengthen and protect you from the evil one.
—2 Thessalonians 3:3

*F*ather God, I pray that You do not take _____ out of this world, but that You protect _____ from the evil one. You are faithful. Strengthen and protect _____ from the evil one. In Jesus's name, I pray. Amen.

——————— ✦ ◆ ✦ ———————

Whispers of Trust to My Wild Child

Dear Wild Child,

Rodeos provide great moments of excitement and laughter. I will never forget your first time attending a rodeo. You were chosen for the mutton-busting event. Do you remember?

The cowboys chose you to participate in trying to ride a lamb. They placed a helmet on your head over your curly brown hair. They straddled you across the woolly creature's back and wrapped your thin arms around its neck. With a slap on the rump, it darted across the arena. You clung to the lamb with tenacious determination but

157

soon rolled underneath the belly and onto the smelly rodeo dirt. You have never liked sheep or trusted cowboys since then.

My child, I realize you do not trust my advice in your life, either. I admit I have made mistakes. As you grew into an adult, I did not know how to react or respond to the diffident attitude you adopted toward me. You see, I did not trust you to make your own decisions. I did not want to see you make the same mistakes I made. So I forced my opinions on you.

I ask you to forgive me, and let us begin to renew a relationship of trust. Instead of trying to boss you around, I am simply going to pray for the Good Shepherd to carry you close to His heart. We can both trust Him.

He tends his flock like a shepherd: He gathers the lambs in his arms and carries them close to his heart; he gently leads those that have young.
—Isaiah 40:11

Jesus, our Good Shepherd, tend Your lamb, _____. Gather _____ as a lamb in Your arms and carry _____ _____ close to Your heart. Lead me gently as I trust my child; trusting You, and Your will for _____. In Your name, Jesus. Amen.

◆ ◆ ◆

13

Whispers of Understanding

Issues and Tissues

My Lord, we could have bought stock in tissues. My daughter's personality presents many issues. Daily, we delve into a box of tissues as she sobs about unseen issues in her life. I say *unseen* because we have not pinpointed why she remains so upset.

My first thought was: *drama queen?* But then I wondered: *bipolar disorder?* Possibly. I do not yet know for sure. What I *do* know is that my daughter cannot seem to contain the emotional chaos. Her moods swing from low to rock bottom. Though I try to understand, I do not fathom to what depths of despair she travels.

I admit it; sometimes I wonder, *What guilt and shame has she hidden that causes such intense despair?*

We have tried professional counseling, but it has not relieved her pain. Indeed, it has actually accentuated her desolation. Now I watch for suicidal signs. My heart aches with helplessness. I am at a loss to understand or meet her needs.

I lean on the Lord God when I hear the wails begin. Thankfully, He understands my daughter's issues. He holds her thoughts; I hold her tightly and help hand her the tissues to soak up her tears, trusting in God's greatness alone for her healing.

He heals the brokenhearted and binds up their wounds. He determines the number of the stars and calls them each by name. Great is our Lord and mighty in power; his understanding has no limit.
—Psalm 147:3–5

*L*ord Jesus, hold _____'s broken heart and bind up her wounds. You determine the number of the stars and call them each by name. You are great, Lord! Show Yourself mighty in power in _____'s life. Touch _____'s heart with the knowledge that Your understanding of her has no limit. In Your name, I pray, Jesus. Amen.

◆ ◆ ◆

The Needy One

This special child always held unique needs. Immature emotionally and undeveloped physically, he never played well with other children. Bullied by both boys and girls, my child withdrew into himself. He pretended to be invisible. With stealth, he walked to and from school, attempting to hide from classmates.

No one understood my child. The counselor suggested my child might have a slight case of autism. "No," the doctor said, "your child needs counseling."

Desperate, I sought therapy, medication, and special education. I spent money. Time revolved around the needs of the special child. Enormous amounts of energy surged out of me to protect my little one from classmates' abuse.

Still today, no one yet understands. My child is withdrawn and isolated. He does not fit in. He cannot conform to the dictates of adolescent social acceptance. A hard shell of unfriendliness covers up the need for acceptance by others. He still seeks invisibility.

Yet I witness the confusion and bitterness within his eyes. I know there is only one Person who understands my child's needs. Now I expend my energy on my knees in prayer for God to be the refuge of love and acceptance for my special child.

You have been a refuge for the poor, a refuge for the needy in his distress, a shelter from the storm and a shade from the heat. For the breath of the ruthless is like a storm driving against a wall.
—Isaiah 25:4

*F*ather, be a refuge for _____. _____ is needy and in distress. My child needs a shelter from the storm and a shade from the heat. For the breath of the ruthless is like a storm driving _____ against a wall. God, become a refuge of love and acceptance for _____. I ask this in the name of Your Son, Jesus. Amen.

◆ ◆ ◆

Sin Tsunami

My wild child's rebellion wreaks havoc. Earthquakes of revolt rattle his finances, relationships, and personal peace. Tsunami waves of consequence flood over him. He struggles to stay afloat in his self-made sea of revolution.

My son searches for fulfillment in sin. He ignores the reality of sin's vengeance; the vengeance that squelches the quietness of peace within a human soul. He opts for devilry over righteousness, anarchy over tranquility.

My child declares he is a Christ follower. Yet no fruitful evidence is present. Does he not understand Scripture?

"He must turn from evil and do good; he must seek peace and pursue it. For the eyes of the Lord are on the righteous and his ears are attentive to their prayer, but the face of the Lord is against those who do evil."
—1 Peter 3:11–12

Thankfully, I am not ignorant of God's Word. I will pray for my son to accept the Lord's righteousness and peace into his troubled life. My petitions will go before the Most High God, who alone grants quietness in the midst of turmoil—the quietness only He can engineer within.

The fruit of righteousness will be peace; the effect of righteousness will be quietness and confidence forever. My people will live in peaceful dwelling places, in secure homes, in undisturbed places of rest.
—Isaiah 32:17–18

*F*ather, let _____ experience that the fruit of righteousness is peace. Let _____ understand that the effect of righteousness is quietness and confidence forever. I ask for _____ to live in peaceful dwelling places and in a secure home. Grant _____ undisturbed places of rest. I ask this in Your Son's name. Amen.

———————— ◆ ◆ ◆ ————————

Thorns of Beauty

*H*er beauty startles passersby, as both genders remark on her exquisite allure. From the time she could toddle, people would stop me to comment on her extraordinary beauty. Indeed, the splendor of her appearance hinders her from normal interaction with others. Some men may lust and some women envy.

My daughter, weary of being examined and spotlighted for her physical attributes, is now tormented by her beauty; it is a thorn in her side. In angry revenge, she has decided to use it for her benefit and to hurt others.

Narcissism now replaces concern for others. Provocative piercings substitute for the gold band once worn to symbolize purity. Sexual innuendos send messages of temptations. Promises of promiscuity lure men into her web of retaliation. She calculates her friendships with women based on how they fawn over her.

Although she does not realize it, her beauty and charm are fading. The thorn of beauty threatening to pierce my daughter's inner loveliness. My heart rends as I try to persuade her to accept her blessings, without making it her whole identity. My child needs to understand that beauty comes from within, not from physical attractiveness.

Charm is deceptive, and beauty is fleeting; but a woman who fears the Lord is to be praised. Give her the reward she has earned, and let her works bring her praise at the city gate.
—Proverbs 31:30–31

*O*h Father God, let _____ realize that sexual charm is deceptive and harmful. Although she is young, I pray _____ can somehow understand that her beauty is fleeting. (This I know for certain!) Embed in _____ the knowledge that a woman who fears the Lord is to be praised. Let _____ somehow understand this truth, regardless of what our culture dictates about beauty and charm. In Jesus's name. Amen.

◆ ◆ ◆

Fruitcakes

Last Christmas, I received an edible fruitcake gift. People really do give them! I knew jokes abounded about the one fruitcake

163

that everyone just keeps regifting. Then, it actually showed up on my doorstep. What comprises a fruitcake?

Once I unboxed the loaf, I was amazed at what appeared to be in this leaden cake. Hard chunks of gleaming candied fruits. Riddled with chopped nuts. The rum odor wafting through plastic wrap. It did not, in the least, look appealing to my taste.

That's my wild child's presentation—an unappealing, fruitcake sort of mix. So full of himself that prideful looks and haughty remarks float out of him as easily as the whiff of rum from the fruitcake. No one can speak to him that he does not consider below him. He is nutty with illusions of grandeur. Where once a sweet kid resided, now lives an intolerable, conceited bore.

I lacked appreciation for the colorful rum-soaked loaf that appeared at my house, tasteless to me. I do not enjoy the arrogant kid who lives in my home. However, though I was not grateful for the Christmas fruitcake, I am very thankful for my child that God can remove tasteless pride from people.

"When my sanity returned to me, so did my honor and glory and kingdom....

"Now I, Nebuchadnezzar, praise and glorify and honor the King of heaven. All his acts are just and true, and he is able to humble those who are proud."
—Daniel 4:36–37 (NLT)

_L_ord God, restore _____'s sanity, removing the pride and rebellion against You. Let my child, _____, praise and glorify and honor You, the King of heaven. Teach _____ that You resist and humble those who are proud and that all Your acts are just and true. In Jesus's name. Amen.

◆ ◆ ◆

Artsy Persuasion

Pastel chalk decorated our driveway. Finger paints speckled our floors. Watercolor pictures graced our fridge. My child's artistic flair developed early in life and continued to refine itself as the years slipped by: he worked with wood and his hands molded gold, silver, and precious stones.

From where did my son derive the artsy gene? I tried to figure it out. Certainly was not from me; I cannot even draw recognizable stick figures. Besides not inheriting the art talent from me, he also did not inherit my temperament. I am type-A personality—let's get it done and now! My son is laid-back, likes to chill out, and wonders, *What's the rush?*

He also lends himself to heavy marijuana use. This, combined with my son's laid-back attitude and his ingenuity in the arts, means that he lazes around smoking drugs and visualizing his next masterpiece. Unfortunately, he never finishes a project. He loses interest. The artwork disappears into a closet where darkness shrouds its vibrant color and design.

God bestowed on my son a natural ability to create beauty. Yet my child smokes away the talent, ambition, and potential to make something for the glory of God. Nevertheless, my wild child's smoky haze does not hinder our Creator from being able to craft my son into a masterpiece for His glory.

"And he has filled him with the Spirit of God, with skill, ability and knowledge in all kinds of crafts—to make artistic designs for work in gold, silver and bronze, to cut and set stones, to work in wood and to engage in all kinds of artistic craftsmanship."
—Exodus 35:31–33

Lord God, fill _____ with the Spirit of God, skill, ability, and knowledge in all kinds of crafts. Let _____'s

165

art bring glory to You when he/she makes artistic designs of gold and silver. Enable _____ to work in wood and to engage in all kinds of artistic craftsmanship, so others will praise Your name. In Jesus's name. Amen.

◆ ◆ ◆

Chip Off the Old Block

My son is just like his father in so many ways. He defines the term *chip off the old block*. Both father and son work in the field of construction. They are rough and tough men. They drink alcohol, shoot pool, swear, and carouse. They think religion is for sissies.

Pride fills my heart that my son is a man's man, but I long for him to become a man of God, too—a man of God who works hard and has a good time but follows in the footsteps of Jesus. I want my child to be a chip off the old block all right, but I pray for him to become a chip off the Rock—Jesus Christ. *"Trust in the LORD forever, for the LORD, the LORD, is the Rock eternal"* (Isaiah 26:4).

The earthly father of my son may influence him for the moment, but I trust that, the influence of our heavenly Father will prevail in my wild child's spiritual life. I pray for both my son and his father to come to know the Father and the Son.

"Therefore everyone who hears these words of mine and puts them into practice is like a wise man who built his house on the rock. The rain came down, the streams rose, and the winds blew and beat against that house; yet it did not fall, because it had its foundation on the rock."
—Matthew 7:24–25

Lord Jesus, open _____'s ears to hear Your words and put them into practice. I pray that _____ will become like the wise man who built his house on the rock. I ask that _____ will be prepared when the rains come down, the streams rise, and the winds blow and beat against his/her house. I pray that _____ will not fall, because he/she has his/her foundation in You, the Rock. In Your name, I pray. Amen.

◆ ◆ ◆

Guilt Massage

Waves of guilt wash rhythmically over my daughter. Cries of an unborn child ring in her ears. At night, she awakens from nightmares of clinical steel and faces of detached emotion. She endures a massage of guilt every day.

I am incapable of understanding the emotional turmoil my daughter is going through. I beg her to seek post-abortion counseling, but she refuses. Her shame prevents her from confessing her physical and emotional experience. She says, "I can't even look in the mirror, let alone admit my sin in front of someone else."

My heart breaks and I speak truisms. "God will forgive you. Pray and ask for His comfort. He will make something good from this, somehow."

However, the guilt speaks louder. My daughter walks through the day with a haunted look. Occasionally, she rubs her flat belly, and then I hear her heave a sigh of resignation and sadness.

Although the words I speak may even sound to her like clichés, truth still resides in them. If she seeks Jesus, He will show understanding, mercy, and great love. He will massage away her guilt with compassion. Jesus will say to my broken child, *"Daughter, your faith has healed you. Go in peace and be freed from your suffering"* (Mark 5:34).

Remember, O LORD, your great mercy and love, for they are from of old. Remember not the sins of my youth and my

167

rebellious ways; according to your love remember me, for you are good, O LORD. Good and upright is the LORD; therefore he instructs sinners in his ways.
—Psalm 25:6–8

O Lord, remember Your great mercy and love, for they are from old. Remember not the sins and rebellious ways of my child, _____. According to Your love for _____, remember him/her, for You are good, O Lord. You are good and upright; therefore instruct _____ in Your ways. In Jesus's name. Amen.

◆ ◆ ◆

Waif

*M*y darling daughter believes Hollywood lies, such as, "Thin is in!" She wants to be waifish. The desire for extreme thinness drives my daughter to exercise herself to exhaustion. She refuses to eat. On the rare occasions she does accept a few bites of nourishment, she rushes into the bathroom to purge.

Although she acknowledges Jesus Christ as her Savior, she refuses to allow Him to become Lord of her life. Instead, her obsession with thinness sits on the throne of her heart. It rules her life day and night.

She reminds me of the Israelites whom God set free from slavery in Egypt. *"Then believed they his words; they sang his praise. They soon forgat his works; they waited not for his counsel: but lusted exceedingly in the wilderness, and tempted God in the desert. And he gave them their request; but sent leanness into their soul"* (Psalm 106:12–15 KJV).

My daughter will not wait for the counsel and healing of the Lord God. She lusts after thinness. Not only is she starving-thin, but also my child has a leanness in her soul. She is unfilled spiritually, emotionally, and physically.

I cannot force her to open her mouth and eat, but I can pray for the Bread of life to fill her with health and wholeness again.

Oh, Bread of life, allow my little waif to taste of Your truth about her leanness of the soul and physical thinness. Fill her to fullness.

I am the LORD your God, who brought you up out of Egypt. Open wide your mouth and I will fill it.
—Psalm 81:10

*O*h Lord God, I ask that _____ recognize that You are the Lord, his/her God. Let _____ understand that You can bring him/her out of the bondage of his/her Egypt. Help _____ to open wide his/her mouth so that You can fill it. In Jesus's name. Amen.

◆ ◆ ◆

Whispers of Understanding to My Wild Child

Dear Wild Child,

Oh my beloved child, how I love you! The moment I first held you in my arms, my life's purpose changed forever. My heart melted the moment you nuzzled against my breast. Swaddled in the soft baby blanket, you snatched my self-absorption and replaced it with consuming concern for your well-being.

I realize that you cannot understand my pushing, pulling, and prodding you toward Jesus. I need you to know that, in my mother's heart, nothing is more important than for you to discover all the wonderful things that Christ offers to those who seek Him. I want to remind you: *"The LORD is wonderfully good to those who wait for him and seek him"* (Lamentations 3:25 NLT). Do you remember memorizing this and receiving that coveted summer pass to the water park? I wanted to embed the truth of the verse with a tangible reward.

I identify with your rebellion. Rebellion seems to reside in our family heritage. Nevertheless, obstinate hearts are a mother's specialty. It is my purpose to encourage your heart, mind, and soul to seek the treasures Christ freely offers.

I will never give up on this. It is a life purpose I want to fulfill with all my love.

My purpose is that they may be encouraged in heart and united in love, so that they may have the full riches of complete understanding, in order that they may know the mystery of God, namely, Christ, in whom are hidden all the treasures of wisdom and knowledge.
—Colossians 2:2–3

*L*ord Jesus, my purpose in prayer is that _____ may be encouraged in heart and united in love with You, so that _____ may have the full riches of complete understanding, in order that _____ may know the mystery of God, namely Christ, in whom are hidden all the treasures of wisdom and knowledge. In Your name. Amen.

———————— ◆ ◆ ◆ ————————

14

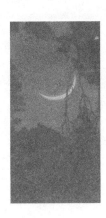

Whispers of Safety

Dangerous Games

Blood red and jet black clothing inhabits my son's closet. Suspicion arises within me, and I suspect my child is toying around with a gang. I study his actions closely, noticing code words whispered to friends and attempts to hide hand signals as we walk through the store. Friends appear and then cluster together.

My son swears he is not part of a gang.

However, I recognize the aloneness my child has faced. Ridiculed by classmates, my child became shy. He battled academically, because teachers were indifferent to his learning disabilities. His father ignores him in exchange for the thrill of business pursuits. The youth clique at church regards him as an outsider.

My child wants to belong. He needs to feel a part of something. Has my child found acceptance in gang involvement? If yes, danger lurks for him physically, emotionally, and spiritually.

I do not know what to do, except to trust in the Lord. I once heard someone say, "Never be afraid to trust an unknown future to a known God." This statement fits my fears and hopes. I fear for my son, yet I trust in the Lord. Yes, my son's future—his safety, must be placed in the Lord God Almighty's hands. Only He can keep my son from participating in the gangs' dangerous games.

The name of the LORD is a strong tower; the righteous run to it and are safe.
—Proverbs 18:10

*O*h Father, steer _____ away from any unsavory gang involvement. Let Your name become the strong tower where _____ finds his solace. Teach _____ to be righteous and to use Your name as a place of safety. In Your name, I pray. Amen.

———————— ◆ ◆ ◆ ————————

Dinner Calling

A chair sits vacant. An unspoken void fills the atmosphere, although chitchat about the day's events floats around the dinner table. I pause a moment to wonder, *Where is my child? With whom is she eating?*

The *"sinners"* who ate with Jesus did not dine at their mother's table either. Surely, those moms ached with emptiness for their wayward children. They heard the taunts from self-righteous people about their child: "Sinner! The parents must have done something wrong." "Tax collector! And from such a good family!"

Especially at mealtimes, when families gather to share their day, hurt envelopes the hearts of parents whose children mutiny against family and faith. Yet Jesus came not for the righteous, but for the sinner. Does He not come to dine with each of us and us with him, and call us to righteousness every day?

Although I have no idea where my child dines tonight, Jesus does. Moreover, even if my child does not recognize Him, Christ sits quietly at the table to watch over my wayward child.

When the teachers of the law who were Pharisees saw him eating with the "sinners" and tax collectors, they asked his disciples: "Why does he eat with tax collectors and 'sinners'?"

On hearing this, Jesus said to them, "It is not the healthy who need a doctor, but the sick. I have not come to call the righteous, but sinners."

—Mark 2:16–17

*J*esus, no matter where my prodigal child, _____, may eat tonight, protect him/her with Your presence. Call _____ to righteousness and lead my child away from sin. In Your name, I pray. Amen.

◆ ◆ ◆

Zipline

Rebellion punctuates every activity in my son's life. He risks his life by refusing to use any common sense in the most dangerous stunts. He taunts me with his actions, "I'll show you!" when I voice the least concern for his safety.

I sigh as he heads out the door. Only God knows where he is headed to experience the next "extreme sport." He refuses to use a helmet, guards, or any type of device developed for safety.

Does my son have any common sense? I find myself wondering. *Does he do it to spite me? Does he think he is invincible?* All three of these issues probably apply to my son's foolish behavior.

I relate to Proverbs 10:1: *"A wise son brings joy to his father, but a foolish son grief to his mother."* A helpless anxiety within me burns, fueled by fear and grief at my son's lack of wisdom. . If my son were to use the slightest wisdom—as he used to display before he rebelled with his kamikaze exploits—joy would infuse me! But what can I do? He is of age. I can no longer rule over his decisions.

Therefore, as his mom, I mentally attach him to the zipline of God's wisdom and sovereignty. I stand back, breathe deeply, and allow God's invisible hand to protect him through this foolish season of life.

"Hold on tight to my son, Lord; hold on tight," I whisper aloud.

Do not forsake wisdom, and she will protect you; love her, and she will watch over you.
—Proverbs 4:6

*A*lmighty God, let this scary season of foolishness pass quickly in _____'s life. Bring wisdom back into his life. Protect _____ until he grows out of his rebellion and into wisdom again. But Lord, in the meantime, keep _____ tied to Your zipline of safety. In Jesus's name, amen.

◆ ◆ ◆

Poles

The preschool called and said my little girl had broken her arm. I rushed over and found her in the nurse's room. Hunched over and holding her tiny arm, she sobbed, "My arm broke!"

I gathered her in my arms, and we hurried to the hospital emergency room.

"What happened, honey?" I asked as we sped down the highway.

"I go down fire pole."

Finally, after further questioning, I understood. The playground had a fire pole the kids slid down. Instead of grabbing and sliding, she lunged and missed the pole altogether. She landed in a crumpled heap, her arm on the bottom.

Sadly, she still likes poles. But, now she slithers up and down the poles. Barely clothed, she pole dances to earn a sizable income. Her delicate arms entangle the pole while she entices lust-filled men for additional tips.

I want my girl to dance, but to dance in honor of the Lord as King David did in 2 Samuel 6:14: *"David, wearing a linen ephod, danced before the LORD with all his might."*

I yearn for my wild child to lose her fascination with poles (unless, it is a fishing pole) and for her to clothe herself with linen of any type. I desire for my daughter to return unharmed by this terrible fall into the world of lust.

For the LORD your God moves about in your camp to protect you and to deliver your enemies to you. Your camp must be holy, so that he will not see among you anything indecent and turn away from you.
—Deuteronomy 23:14

*O*h, Lord God, move about in _____'s life. Protect _____ and deliver _____ from this life of sin. Impress on _____ that his/her life must be holy and that You, Lord God, do not want to see anything indecent in his/her life. In Jesus's name. Amen.

———— ◆ ◆ ◆ ————

Fireproof

The local evening news replayed the clip of the smoldering ruins of the $20 million dollar condominium project. Not one piece of lumber remained—only heaps of rubble. Ashes floated through the air. Over the city, the acrid smell of smoke lingered. The building was destroyed by fire. Someone's hard work had been incinerated.

I watch my child as she parties through life; busy all the time, but not building anything that will last for eternity. She carouses every night of the week. Then my daughter drags in to work with a hangover, does her job, and then hurries to the next social gig.

My child fritters time and money on her hair, nails, and clothing. These normal girly routines consume her to the point of compulsion. She obsesses on outward appearance, so she can impress her "friends" that congregate at the clubs every night.

My child's relationship with God has vanished. I see no evidence that she even thinks about anything other than the next carousel. The promiscuous fire of clubbing with her friends has extinguished her spiritual life.

I worry. Life is so short, just a mist, as James wrote: *"Why, you do not even know what will happen tomorrow. What is your life? You are a mist that appears for a little while and then vanishes"* (James 4:14). I want my daughter's life to count for something. But more importantly, I desire her to be fireproofed for eternity. Only a relationship with Jesus Christ can keep her safe.

> *If what he has built survives, he will receive his reward. If it is burned up, he will suffer loss; he himself will be saved, but only as one escaping through the flames.*
> —1 Corinthians 3:14–15

$\mathcal{L}$ord Jesus, show _____ what she is building with her life. Remind _____ that there will be an eternal reward. Lord, I pray that _____ will be saved, if only as one escaping through the flames. In Your name, I pray. Amen.

———————— ◆ ◆ ◆ ————————

Camouflage

$\mathcal{O}$live-green toy soldiers lined the shelves. Worn and torn camouflage costumes stashed in dresser drawers were worn at bedtime. *Rat-a-tat, rat-a-tat* sounded through our home as our son pretended to be an army commander. My little boy loved military history and war movies. He considered the army his only career option.

He graduated high school and then boot camp. He excelled in survival training. Bull's-eye target practice came naturally to my sharpshooter. My son proudly wore his camouflage uniform for his country.

He marched with his military orders for war deployment but came home depleted of emotion. Overseas, he struggled with finding the goodness of God in the blood and guts of war. When he dodged sniper bullets, he doubted the divine Deity of his childhood. When a car bomb exploded and killed his buddies, he jumped ship on Jesus. *How could a loving God allow this?* he questioned.

My son no longer wears camouflage. However, I am praying he becomes a warrior again. I pray that my child once again dons the uniform of faith.

Stand firm then, with the belt of truth buckled around your waist, with the breastplate of righteousness in place, and with your feet fitted with the readiness that comes from the gospel of peace. In addition to all this, take up the shield of faith, with which you can extinguish all the flaming arrows of the evil one. Take the helmet of salvation and the sword of the Spirit, which is the word of God.
—Ephesians 6:14–17

*L*ord Jesus, teach _____ to stand firm, with the belt of truth buckled around his/her waist, with the breastplate of righteousness in place. Fit the feet of _____ with the readiness that comes from the gospel of peace. In addition, give ____ _____ the shield of faith with which he/she can extinguish all the flaming arrows of the evil one. Enable _____ to put on the helmet of salvation and to use the sword of the Spirit, which is the Word of God. In Your name, Jesus. Amen.

❖ ◆ ❖

Obstacle Course

At youth camp, my child's favorite activity was the obstacle course. He would run it repeatedly. He liked the challenge. The competition of the event pushed him to the limit of his abilities. He desired to win the trophy, a goal he usually accomplished. He took pride in the triumph.

After a week at camp, my son would bound off the bus. He jabbered all the way home about "this year's obstacle course." As soon as he unloaded his smelly unwashed clothes into the laundry room, he would head out to the backyard to attempt to build a close replica of the newer course. After dinner, he would proudly walk me out to the backyard to display his labor of love.

Funny how things change, yet they stay the same. Although my son is now an adult, he still struggles with obstacles and pride. The obstacles are different now: challenges from colleagues, climbing the corporate ladder, or building a solid relationship with his wife. Nevertheless, the pride remains the same. He takes credit for every success and strives to remove the obstacles of life by his own merit. He will not admit that he needs help from the hand of God.

Yes, my wild child is still running an obstacle course, but it is not in a spiritual way. However, until he swallows his pride, he will not win the trophy.

"Build up, build up, prepare the road! Remove the obstacles out of the way of my people." For this is what the high and lofty One says— he who lives forever, whose name is holy: "I live in a high and holy place, but also with him who is contrite and lowly in spirit, to revive the spirit of the lowly and to revive the heart of the contrite."
—Isaiah 57:14–15

*L*ord God, say, "Build up, build up, prepare the road! Remove the obstacles out of the way of _____." You are the high and lofty One who lives forever and whose name is Holy. Help _____ have a contrite and lowly spirit. In Jesus's name. Amen.

◆ ◆ ◆

Scamp

Define *scamp*? Well, my child models the primary definition of rascal or rogue. However, *Merriam-Webster's American English Dictionary* goes on to define the verb form of *scamp*: "to perform in hasty, neglectful, or imperfect manner." Yes, my child qualifies as a scamp.

Mischief plagues my child each day. Even when he was a tot, he found trouble or trouble found him. For my sanity, we started to attend church regularly. My pastor counseled, "Try reading James Dobson's book, *The Strong-Willed Child*; perhaps that will help." My scamp would have made James Dobson weep.

We visited the hospital emergency room frequently for his mishaps. Our "friend," the emergency room nurse, said half jokingly, "Gee, maybe you should just rent a back room here." My scamp could not be contained anywhere—he could always wiggle out somehow.

However, no matter what I call my child—scamp, rascal, imp, or Mr. Mischief—I know he loves the Lord Jesus Christ. Does he act it out? No! Does he want to behave better? Sometimes. Does God know what is in my child's heart? Yes. *"The LORD does not look at the things man looks at. Man looks at the outward appearance, but the LORD looks at the heart"* (1 Samuel 16:7).

Therefore, no matter how you define the word *scamp*, God sees in my wild child someone who loves Him, but just cannot seem to get his act together. God will be a refuge for both of us; a refuge for a mother's

179

sanity and source of shelter from the local emergency rooms for my scamp's mischievous mishaps.

"Because he loves me," says the LORD, "I will rescue him; I will protect him, for he acknowledges my name."
—Psalm 91:14

𝒟ear Lord, _____ loves You. I pray for You to say, "I will rescue _____; I will protect _____ for he/she acknowledges my name." I pray in Jesus's name. Amen.

———————— ◆ ◆ ◆ ————————

Song of Safety

Musicians hear things differently than nonmusical folks. Their ears differentiate between notes, keys, and beats. But for people like me, it all blends in beautiful music. I adore music, but I admit I am tone deaf, cannot clap to the beat, nor hear the harmony.

On the other hand, my daughter inundates herself in the chords of composition. Music is a god to her. She worships music. My child composes melodies with all her heart, soul, and mind. Lyrical words filter throughout her everyday conversations.

Her obsession with music takes her into a foreign world of nightclubs and lounges. She plays for happiness. She sings for joy. Sometimes she even earns a little income to help tide her over until the next gig.

I feel concern for my daughter's safety. Men come on to her while she performs. Cocaine and methamphetamines are regular visitors at the places where my daughter entertains. Whiskey and beer loosen up inhibitions of the performers and customers. Furthermore, she is not always safe when she hauls her instruments to the car in the wee hours of the morning.

I acknowledge that the Lord gave her gifts and talents, but oh, how I want her to play for Him. I want her to sing songs with lyrics and harmony that worship the Lord God. I want her to seek refuge in Jesus, instead of her music.

But let all who take refuge in you be glad; let them ever sing for joy. Spread your protection over them, that those who love your name may rejoice in you.
—Psalm 5:11

*L*ord God, let _____ learn to take refuge in You. Let _____ learn to be glad in You. Let _____ sing for joy. Spread Your protection over _____ so that _____ may love Your name and rejoice in You. In Jesus's name. Amen.

———————— ◆ ◆ ◆ ————————

Whispers of Safety to My Wild Child

Dear Wild Child,

Your safety dominates my thoughts. At times, my thoughts stray to the what-ifs. What if you are hurt in an accident? What if you destroy your brain cells with alcohol and drugs? What if the significant person in your life turns out to be abusive?

However, my biggest fear is your safety for eternity. Everything that can harm you will be temporary on this earth. However, eternity is. We are promised, *"He will remove all of their sorrows, and there will be no more death or sorrow or crying or pain. For the old world and its evils are gone forever"* (Revelation 21:4 NLT).

I need to know that you have placed your faith in the Savior Jesus Christ. That way, I can look forward to spending *forever* with you in heaven. (Now don't grimace at the thought of being with me for all eternity!)

181

My dear child, come to the arms of God where you will find eternal safety and comfort. This world can be harsh, but we have a better place prepared for us—a new heaven and a new earth.

But in keeping with his promise we are looking forward to a new heaven and a new earth, the home of righteousness. So then, dear friends, since you are looking forward to this, make every effort to be found spotless, blameless and at peace with him. Bear in mind that our Lord's patience means salvation.
—2 Peter 3:13–15

Father God, I am looking forward to Your promise of a new heaven and a new earth—a home of righteousness. Father, open the eyes of _____ to look forward to the same promise. Teach _____ to make every effort to be found spotless, blameless, and at peace with You. In Jesus's name. Amen.

15

Whispers of Faith

Rat Tales

My child chooses to live in squalor. The drug-infested community supports my child's mind-set of illegal substance abuse. The drug dealers and addicts tell tales of delusion. Rats, human-type and rodent-kind, make outlandish roommates for a child raised in a nice home. Together they scrounge for food that is fit only for rodent species. My eyes cannot believe what they see!

Questions run through my mind: *How much lower can my child go before he comes to his senses? How much longer will it be before he turns and comes home? How much longer must I wait?*

Oh, but my faith ensures me that my hopes are not in vain. Although I might not be able to see God's hand in the midst of the foulness of my child's lifestyle, He is at work, even in a rats' nest of humanity. I choose to respond as did the prodigal child's father: *"[The prodigal child] finally came to his senses. . . . So he returned home to his father. And while he was still a long distance away, his father saw him coming. Filled with love and compassion, he ran to his son, embraced him, and kissed him"* (Luke 15:17, 20 NLT).

My faith will not waiver, even when my child stubbornly refuses to admit his addictions dictate his lifestyle. I will wait in faith for his

183

lifestyle to become unbearable. I will be the parent who stands and watches for the return of her wild child.

Now faith is being sure of what we hope for and certain of what we do not see.
—Hebrews 11:1

*F*ather, grant me faith to wait for the return of _____. Enable me to wait patiently for my wild child, _____, to come to his/her senses and to come home. I wait in expectation. In Jesus's name. Amen.

◆ ◆ ◆

Power Drink

I pop into our local convenience store for milk. As I pass down the aisle, it amazes me to see the variety of new power drinks that abound in our culture. Sports figures espouse their benefits in aiding athletic performance. Each sip brims with vitamins, minerals, sugar, and sometimes caffeine. Each bottle holds a concoction that will boost even a thirsty sluggard's energy.

It occurs to me that my child thirsts for a power drink. She attempts to quench her dry soul with a mixture of alcohol, drugs, and promiscuity. But she finds only momentary relief for her soul thirst.

Grasping my cold milk carton, I stride past all the colorful bottles holding promises of thirst-quenching attributes. My child needs more than an energy drink. I realize my child needs Jesus Christ. Only in Christ will she discover the eternal power drink. His living water will satiate her desert-dry heart more thoroughly and conveniently than anything this world falsely offers her.

I wish I could force her to take a sip. She only needs a taste to experience the refreshment of the ultimate power drink, the living water of Jesus. However, I cannot force her. All I can do is exhibit its ultimate power in my own life and pray enough splashes on my child that she will want to hold up her own cup to Jesus.

Jesus answered, "Everyone who drinks this water will be thirsty again, but whoever drinks the water I give him will never thirst. Indeed, the water I give him will become in him a spring of water welling up to eternal life."
—John 4:13–14

𝓛ord Jesus, pour out Your living water on _____'s dry spirit. Help _____ to realize that when he/she drinks of Your water of life, his/her soul will never thirst again. Indeed, the water you give _____ will become a spring of water welling up to eternal life. In Your name, I pray. Amen.

◆ ◆ ◆

Reality Restored

My daughter stares at me with eyes of madness. Distorted reality rules her world. She distrusts everything that I say. She refuses to seek help.

"Nothing is wrong with me!" she screams while her life spirals downward into insanity. "Leave me alone, leave me alone—just leave!"

She lunges toward me. I calmly hold up my hand and back away.

My daughter retreats back into her room, muttering unintelligible words.

I turn away with a sigh of resignation. *Is it drug abuse? Does a chemical imbalance overrule the rational thought process? Could it be schizophrenia? Is she bipolar?* I ask myself.

I do not know, but the Most High God does. *"Is anything too hard for the LORD?"* (Genesis 18:14). No nothing is too hard for my God. Not even the madness that plagues my daughter day in and day out. I reflect on King Nebuchadnezzar's seven-year struggle with insanity. God restored him to the world of reality. Nebuchadnezzar then praised Him: *"His kingdom endures from generation to generation."*

Yes, God's kingdom endures from generation to generation; this includes my wild-eyed daughter's and mine.

At the end of that time, I, Nebuchadnezzar, raised my eyes toward heaven, and my sanity was restored. Then I praised the Most High; I honored and glorified him who lives forever. His dominion is an eternal dominion; his kingdom endures from generation to generation.
—Daniel 4:34

*O*h, my Most High God, help me to remember that nothing is too hard for You. Restore _____'s mind. I wait for the time that _____ raises her eyes toward heaven and praises You with these words, "My sanity was restored. I honor and glorify Him who lives forever." In Jesus's name. Amen.

———————— ◆ ◆ ◆ ————————

Blurred Vision

My child resembles John Lennon. Wire-framed glasses perch across his Roman-straight nose. Long, dirty, blond hair drapes his goateed face. My son emulates John Lennon. He lounges around playing a guitar and writing music with words that make little sense to anyone but him. He calls it "poetic musical art."

Unfortunately, my son's spiritual eyes are blurred also. They do not see Jesus Christ as the Son of God—the world's Savior. They visualize

Him as a good teacher. "Jesus said some cool stuff, man. I wish I could compose like He taught," says my spiritually impaired child. To him, Jesus Christ is a historic figure who holds no impact on today's world events. (*Hmmm. That is just the way I feel about John Lennon.*)

My desire is for my child to resemble Jesus Christ. Jesus probably wore long hair. He sang psalms and hymns with His buddies, the disciples. Might He have played a guitar-type lyre? Jesus knew He was the Son of the Living God—the Savior of the world. I want my child to comprehend this about Jesus too.

Thankfully, I know Jesus can straighten out anyone's poor spiritual eyesight. Just a touch of His hand and maybe a little of the Spirit's spit and my child will see everything clearly. My child will recognize Jesus not as a man walking, but as the risen Christ.

When he had spit on the man's eyes and put his hands on him, Jesus asked, "Do you see anything?"

He looked up and said, "I see people; they look like trees walking around."

Once more Jesus put his hands on the man's eyes. Then his eyes were opened, his sight was restored, and he saw everything clearly.
—Mark 8:23–25

*L*ord Jesus, put Your hands on _____. Open _____'s spiritually blind eyes. Allow _____ to see clearly the reality and truth of Your lordship. I pray this in Your name. Amen.

◆ ◆ ◆

The Carnival

The smell of grilled hot dogs, cotton candy, and grease assault my nostrils. A sunburned man bids me come play the game: "Always a winner!" he says. The heat of sun and noise of whirring rides make me feel slightly light-headed and nauseous.

However, I continue the hunt for my adult son. I wonder, *Why would he choose to live in a place like this?*

After I roam block after block across the hot asphalt and gravel, I spot my son hunched over, holding a wrench. Apparently, The Screamer needs a little repair before the neon lights come on and people pay to ride it.

How scary is that? I think to myself.

My son glances up as my shadow falls across him.

"Hi!" I say.

"Hey," he responds.

"Like to go to church and out to lunch tomorrow?" I ask.

"Mom, you know I am not going to church. Besides, Sunday is the busiest day for us."

"Well, I thought perhaps..."

"No."

I drop the subject. We chitchat a few minutes, and then he says, closing the conversation, "The Screamer is a beaut, isn't she? I'm her ride jock. I gotta go."

My son's life has crumbled into the carnival life. His joy is to grease the gears of a rickety ride. He lost his faith between our home and the carnival midway. However, I know the Restorer of Ruined Lives. He fixes broken people. Everyone always wins with Jesus.

> *"Your people will rebuild the ancient ruins and will raise up the age-old foundations; you will be called Repairer of Broken Walls, Restorer of Streets with Dwellings.... then you will*

find your joy in the LORD, and I will cause you to ride on the heights."
—Isaiah 58:12, 14

*F*ather God, rebuild the ruins of _____'s life. Raise up the age-old foundations of faith in _____. Be the *"Repairer of Broken Walls"* in _____. Restore _____ to You. Then _____ will find joy in You, Lord, causing him to ride to great heights. In Jesus's name. Amen.

—————————— ◆ ◆ ◆ ——————————

Mirage

My child joined a cult today. She performed the necessary rituals, so she is an official member.

I do not understand why my child would choose a religion of good works over the truth of Jesus Christ's grace of forgiveness. Why is my daughter striving for heaven on her own impossible efforts instead of accepting the work of Christ on the Cross as the finished work that it is? By Jesus's grace, it is not *do*, but it is *done: "It is finished"* (John 19:30).

A mirage lures my child into a false religion. The cult's leaders fill her with false hope of what is to come. The false prophets speak what is in their own minds for their own profit. They command; she obeys.

What hope does she have in her own good deeds? The illusion of "achieving heaven" will always be one step ahead of her accomplishments. It is an effort in futility.

Thankfully, my Lord is the Light of the world. He dispels the darkness of lies: *"I am the light of the world. Whoever follows me will never walk in darkness, but will have the light of life"* (John 8:12).

He will disperse the mirage of my daughter's false religion. Someday, she will accept the living water of grace, instead of a cult's impossible demands.

*This is what the LORD Almighty says: "Do not listen to what the
prophets are prophesying to you; they fill you with false hopes.
They speak visions from their own minds, not from the mouth
of the LORD."*
—Jeremiah 23:16

*O*h Lord, I pray that _____ will not listen to today's
"prophets," but only to You. Do not let others fill _____
with false hopes. They speak of visions from their own minds, not the
truth of Your mouth. Teach _____ to recognize the
insincerity of those he/she is listening to each day. In Jesus's name.
Amen.

———————— ◆ ◆ ◆ ————————

Glitter of Gold

The glitter of gold decorates my son's body. Gold earrings, necklaces,
and watches adorn him like a Christmas tree. The sun dances off
the gold that embellishes the car he drives. The interior design of his
office sparkles with golden fixtures, trophies, and desk accessories.

I pray my child's obsession with the wealth of the world will soon
diminish. Materialism draws him away from the Lord Jesus. At this
time, my son places his trust in his prosperity. So far, life has not been
too hard on my child.

However, I know hardships will eventually come because that is the
reality of life on earth. My son's halfhearted faith will be tested.

*"I will refine them like silver and test them like gold. They will
call on my name and I will answer them; I will say, 'They are
my people.'"*
—Zechariah 13:9

When the tests come, I yearn for my child's faith to be so strong that nothing—not even the glitter of gold—will deter him from boldly claiming Jesus as Lord.

> *"If we are thrown into the blazing furnace, the God we serve is able to save us from it, and he will rescue us from your hand, O king. But even if he does not, we want you to know, O king, that we will not serve your gods or worship the image of gold you have set up."*
> —Daniel 3:17–18

*L*ord God, demonstrate to _____ that even if he/she should be thrown into a blazing furnace, You are able to save him/her from it. Lord, I ask that _____'s heart be so committed to You that he/she will say to the world, "But even if my God does not rescue me, I want you to know that I will not serve your gods or worship the image of gold you have set up." In Jesus's name, I ask this for my child, _____. Amen.

◆ ◆ ◆

Think Eternal

*D*arwinism dwarfs my child's belief in God. Strange! Somehow my child believes that pond scum is in his genetics. Weird! Evolution evolved. Deity dissolved. Peculiar!

It is beyond my comprehension why anyone would choose this worldview. I do not believe I evolved from a microbe, to a reptile, to a prehistoric ape, to a human being. What is my child thinking? Nature shouts the truth of a Living God who designed and created every aspect of earth.

> *The heavens declare the glory of God; the skies proclaim the work of his hands. Day after day they pour forth speech;*

night after night they display knowledge. There is no speech or
language where their voice is not heard. Their voice goes out
into all the earth, their words to the ends of the world.
—Psalm 19:1–4

My child's ears must be plugged up with Darwin earwax. Fraud! My
child's eyes are blinded by evolution's deceitful blight. Deception!
God created the earth. Evolution evaporates. Hallelujah! Think
eternal. Truth! Creator comprehension! Glory!

He has made everything beautiful in its time. He has also set
eternity in the hearts of men; yet they cannot fathom what God
has done from beginning to end.
—Ecclesiastes 3:11

*L*ord God, You have made everything beautiful in its time. Open
_____'s eyes to see the beauty of Your creation. You
have also set eternity in the hearts of men. Open _____'s
heart to an eternity spent with You. Help _____ to fathom
what You have done from beginning to end. In Jesus's name. Amen.

◆ ◆ ◆

Whispers of Why

Breaking news! A serial rapist appears to be targeting young red-
haired women. Several of the abductions have occurred in high-
traffic shopping areas. The abductor then takes his prey to the forested
outskirts of town to finalize the crime.

My beautiful red-haired daughter flees the room. Hysterical fear
paints her face. The predator committed his crime on her once; she now
lives in terror that he will find her again.

Her trust in God was shattered the day of the rape. The emotional pain supersedes the physical abuse. The doctors, therapists, and our pastor state it will take years for her to regain trust in people and in God. She quakes in fear and shakes her fist at the Lord.

Why then do you tolerate the treacherous? Why are you silent while the wicked swallow up those more righteous than themselves?
—Habakkuk 1:13

I understand her confusion and rage. I am angry too. Nevertheless, my history with the Lord Jesus tells me He will be faithful even through this heartbreak. I do not know how, but I know He will.

On bended knees, I plead for the capture of the rapist.

On bended knees, I implore that my daughter's shattered faith be restored.

On bended knees, I pray for my red-haired girl who whispers, "Why?"

The Sovereign Lord is my strength; he makes my feet like the feet of a deer, he enables me to go on the heights.
—Habakkuk 3:19

*S*overeign Lord, be _____'s strength. Make _____'s feet like the feet of a deer. Enable _____ to go on the heights. In Jesus's name, I pray. Amen.

◆ ◆ ◆

Whispers of Faith to My Wild Child

Dear Wild Child,

I know you struggle with your faith, but I want you to know that everyone doubts, at times. Remember the story of John the Baptist? Do you recall John's statement of faith? He said, *"Look, the Lamb of God, who takes away the sin of the world!"* (John 1:29).

However, even John questioned. Dark thoughts of doubt surfaced in his thoughts as he sat in a gloomy prison cell. He wondered, *Could I have been wrong?* So he sent a couple of his disciples to query Jesus: *"Are you the one who was to come, or should we expect someone else?"* (Matthew 11:3). Although John the Baptist doubted, do not forget what Jesus said about him: *"I tell you the truth: Among those born of women there has not risen anyone greater than John the Baptist; yet he who is least in the kingdom of heaven is greater than he"* (Matthew 11:11).

So do not allow your doubt to override your faith. Grasp your belief in Christ with your heart, mind, and will, realizing that questions will arise.

I confess my faith struggles at times. It is hard to trust an unseen God when everything seems to go awry. Nevertheless, I will tell you that in the times my faith has been the weakest, God has proven most powerful. In hindsight, I now know it is during the bouts of doubt that my faith in Jesus Christ grows stronger.

My child, keep the faith. Believe!

Great is the Lord! He is most worthy of praise! His greatness is beyond discovery! Let each generation tell its children of your mighty acts. I will meditate on your majestic, glorious splendor and your wonderful miracles.
—Psalm 145:3–5 (NLT)

*O*h Lord, You *are* the Lord. You are most worthy of praise. Your greatness is beyond discovery! Let _____ tell his/her children of Your mighty acts. I pray that _____ will meditate on Your majestic, glorious splendor and Your wonderful miracles. In Jesus's name. Amen.

◆ ◆ ◆

16

Whispers of Mercy

Mercy Me!

After work, I pour myself a tall glass of sweetened iced tea with lemon slices floating on top. I plop myself onto the couch for a few minutes of rest. My tired feet stretch across the coffee table. The courtroom television show mesmerizes me for a few nonsensical moments. I reach for the cold refreshment as the verdict is announced. The judge uses acidic comments as she trounces the accused. The onslaught of verbiage is meant to ridicule, humiliate, and accuse the defendant.

The tart taste of the lemon slides across my tongue. At the same time, I realize how sour and dour my own words are with my child. Guilt rises up within me. How many times have I witnessed the look of defeat in my wild child's eyes? I am the judge and jury in our kitchen courtroom. I ridicule and accuse. A guilty verdict is issued and I consider what type of punishment would be worthy of such insidious acts of waywardness.

The sweetness of the iced tea dissolves with the overuse of tangy lemon, the same as my child experiences my harshness, instead of my deep love. My child does not recognize my concern, but hears only my critical spirit. My child experiences judgment, not mercy.

I get up from the couch and switch off the courtroom drama. I dump my tea down the sink, trash the lemons, and refill my glass with only sweet iced tea. This refreshing drink now washes away the lingering sour taste as I determine to use words filled with sweet mercy to wash away previous bitter comments. Mercy will triumph over judgment in this kitchen courtroom.

Mercy triumphs over judgment!
—James 2:13

Father God, teach me that mercy always triumphs over judgment. Please reveal to _____ Your mercy. I pray that other people, me included, will show mercy to _____ and to all the wild children of this world. In Your merciful Son's name. Amen.

◆ ◆ ◆

Journal of Tears

Salty tears stain the pages of my prayer journal. Page after page, inky smears blur the details of wayward rebellion in my child. My heart breaks as I continue to list my prayers for this precious young woman.

What happened to the cherub who crawled onto my lap? Where is the angelic child who whispered bedtime prayers? Gone! Somehow, adolescence burglarized my home. It stole my daughter's innocence and replaced it with reckless behavior in a dominion of darkness.

Tears continue to wet the page. Softly, these words from a psalm whisper in my head: *"You keep track of all my sorrows. You have collected all my tears in your bottle. You have recorded each one in your book"* (Psalm 56:8 NLT). Surely, God sees my tears. He journals my tears, just as I journal the prayers for my daughter. Comfort begins to replace the pain in my heart.

Then another promise unfolds in my mind: *"Those who sow in tears will reap with songs of joy"* (Psalm 126:5). I jot down the verse and write, "Amen!" As I close the damp pages, I whisper, "Lord, out of this journal of tears, reap a harvest of joy and righteousness in my child."

> *And we pray this in order that you may live a life worthy of the Lord and may please him in every way:... being strengthened with all power according to his glorious might so that you may have great endurance and patience, and joyfully giving thanks to the Father, who has qualified you to share in the inheritance of the saints in the kingdom of light. For he has rescued us from the dominion of darkness and brought us into the kingdom of the Son he loves, in whom we have redemption, the forgiveness of sins.*
> —Colossians 1:10–14

Father, I will not stop praying for _____. I ask You to strengthen my child's willpower according to Your glorious might so that my child may have great endurance and patience and joyfully give thanks to You, Father. I pray that _____ will be qualified to share in the inheritance of the saints in the kingdom of light. In Jesus's name. Amen.

———— ◆ ◆ ◆ ————

Rotten Apple

The worm wiggled further into the core of the tart green apple. I gagged. *Ick! What if I ate a part of the squirmy thing?* Upon closer inspection, I could see the worm twist itself further into the core of my fruit.

This is exactly what evil has done to my wild child. The sins began small, and then grew in size. They wormed their way into my child's heart without anyone noticing the decaying rot hidden in the heart of my child's soul. Now my wild child is rotten to the core.

Nonetheless, God is merciful. He loves my child as the apple of His eye. The Lord will create circumstances to bring the worm of evil out of my wild child. Somehow, someway, someday, His Spirit will make my child's heart clean and healthy. God's Word, instead of the worm of evil, will become alive in this wild one. My child will acknowledge the truth of Proverbs 7:2: *"Keep my commands and you will live; guard my teachings as the apple of your eye."*

Yes, my wild child is a rotten apple. God will protect my child and hide him under the shadow of His wings. I believe God will soon turn the worm around because my child is an apple of God's eye.

> *Show me your unfailing love in wonderful ways. You save with your strength those who seek refuge from their enemies. Guard me as the apple of your eye. Hide me in the shadow of your wings.*
> —Psalm 17:7–8 (NLT)

*O*h Lord God, show Your unfailing love to _____. Save _____ with Your strength. Protect my child from further decay from the enemy. Guard _____ as the apple of Your eye. Hide _____ in the shadow of Your wings. In Jesus's name, I pray. Amen.

◆ ◆ ◆

Diva Disgraced

The Sunday paper ran the headline, "Diva Disgraced!" It is only a small hometown newspaper, not a national tabloid. But the phone still jangled all day. Family and friends emailed, asking questions. My diva daughter had disgraced herself in the public eye.

My little diva was always dressed to the nines. She was captain of the varsity volleyball team. She excelled academically, making the dean's list. My diva won the coveted title of homecoming queen. A faithful Christian above all else, she spoke harshly and criticized anyone who did not share her rigid and pharisaical faith. She seemed so straight, she could not turn a corner. However, not now.

I hear her wails of tears. Her perfect persona ruined because she was caught in a compromise with her boyfriend. A cell phone camera caught my daughter's act… Within hours, the scoop flew across the Internet, and now it is front-page news—literally.

I am appalled and embarrassed too. Yet I am grateful for God's faithfulness in my diva daughter's life. The Lord's Word is true: *"Pride goes before destruction, a haughty spirit before a fall"* (Proverbs 16:18). She has tumbled off her self-made pedestal.

My disgraced diva shall discover that she will live through the humiliation. I pray she learns to grasp the truth of her Christian faith, finding meekness and humility, considering others better than herself.

Oh, I pray that others show her mercy too—literally.

He has showed you, O man, what is good. And what does the LORD require of you? To act justly and to love mercy and to walk humbly with your God.
—Micah 6:8

*O*h Father, teach _____ what is good. Show _____ what You require of her. Instruct _____ on how to act justly and to love mercy and to walk humbly with You. In Jesus's name. Amen.

◆ ◆ ◆

Cloudy Days

The rain drips from the roof in synchronized time with my tears falling on the table. Deep gray clouds drift over the horizon, as depression hovers over my heart. It is a gloomy day in my life.

My child disappeared months ago. He packed and left without word. I have not heard from him since then. I did not receive a call on Mother's Day. A card did not arrive by mail for my birthday. I do not anticipate a Christmas gift. My child has abandoned me to walk in rebellion.

All he left me with is fear-filled concern. Is my child all right? Is my child alive? Fears filter through my thoughts during the day. Anxiety thunders through my soul in the deep of night. Will I ever hear from my son again?

Thankfully, I know the God who can guide my son and me through this cloudy season of life. My Lord can guide my child with a pillar of fire through the darkness of sin-filled nights. His mercy will not abandon my child to the hopelessness of rebellion. My Lord's mercy will comfort my heart in this wilderness of painful loss.

My tears cease as I see the sunshine through the clouds. A luminous rainbow sparkles through the peeping sunshine. Yes, the Lord God is filled with great mercy.

But in your great mercy you did not abandon them to die in the wilderness. The pillar of cloud still led them forward by day, and the pillar of fire showed them the way through the night.
—Nehemiah 9:19 (NLT)

*F*ather God, in Your great mercy do not abandon _____ in the wilderness of rebellion. Lead _____ forward in the day and show _____ the way through the darkness of night. Thank You for Your great mercy to both of us. In Jesus's name. Amen.

———————— ◆ ◆ ◆ ————————

Stain Remover

Detergent- and bleach-pens amaze me. When I splatter tomato red spaghetti sauce on my yellow shorts, one touch of the pen and *poof*—it is gone! Or the dribble of coffee on my new white T-shirt vanishes with a dab of a bleach marker. Amazing!

How I wish I owned a large cleansing pen to remove all the blemishes of unrighteousness that my son allows to stain him. Lies, rage, sexual immorality, and an excess of other sins blotch his soul. However, only the Lord Jesus Christ can do that cleansing, and He does it with His crimson-red blood that was shed on the Cross.

I cannot be the laundress of my child's dirt-filled life. Nevertheless, I am able to drop off my cleaning requests to the Lord. Because of His mercy, I can come before His throne on behalf of my child. *"So let us come boldly to the throne of our gracious God. There we will receive his mercy, and we will find grace to help us when we need it"* (Hebrews 4:16 NLT).

So I am dropping off my cleaning list today. I will ask the Lord God, in His mercy, to reason with my sin-stained wild child. My God holds the ultimate stain remover in the palm of His hands.

"Come now, let us reason together," says the Lord. "Though your sins are like scarlet, they shall be as white as snow; though they are red as crimson, they shall be like wool."
—Isaiah 1:18

Lord God, please reason with _____. Let _____ _____ realize that though his/her sins are like scarlet, You make them white as snow. Lord, cleanse _____'s scarlet red sin to make it white as wool. In Jesus's name. Amen.

◆ ◆ ◆

Hurdles

Her long, lean legs raced along the track. Hurdle after hurdle, she led the pack in the hurdle-jumping event. Although I had watched her participate in this event for years, my stomach stilled lurched as she strode toward the next barrier.

Then my fears came to fruition. For a moment, she looked down as she leapt. With her eyes not looking ahead, her white athletic shoes clipped the top edge of the hurdle. She took a face-plant into the gray asphalt track. My daughter looked up startled, surprised, and bleeding. She struggled to her feet and moved backwards to attempt the obstacle again. Success! Now she was no longer in the lead. She finished the event in last place.

I felt sorry for my athlete, but at the same time, I knew there was a biblical object lesson to apply to the unfortunate circumstance.

My daughter teases and ridicules anyone whom she feels is inferior to her, especially Christians. My child believes in doing things her way and doing them independent of God. She shows no mercy for other people's frailties.

I hope that on the way home from the track meet, she will be receptive to a short analogy of her mishap. I think Psalm 25:15 might mean something to her today: *"If I keep my eyes on God, I won't trip over my own feet"* (*The Message*).

Maybe the face-plant will humble her enough to listen to her biggest fan—Mom.

So don't condemn each other anymore. Decide instead to live in such a way that you will not put an obstacle in another Christian's path.
—Romans 14:13 (NLT)

*L*ord Jesus, teach _____ not to condemn others. Encourage _____ to decide instead to live in such a way

that he/she will not put an obstacle in another Christian's path. I pray this in Your name. Amen.

◆ ◆ ◆

Sheepskins

The gamey smell of the sheepskin seat-covers almost overpowers me. They are furry and hot as I slide into the bucket seat. They make me sweat. My daughter purchased these sheepskin seat covers to perk up her yellow convertible. They do not appeal to my taste in interior auto accessories. However, I keep my opinions to myself.

In many ways, my daughter resembles those sheepskins. Her demeanor can be soft and cuddly. On the other hand, she can raise a stink and make me so angry that I sweat profusely while attempting to show her mercy. Nevertheless, I need to demonstrate patience because she is a lost sheep in the kingdom of God.

I choose to show mercy as an avenue to win her over to the Good Shepherd. He showed me mercy rather than condemnation. I desire to reflect to my child the same caring qualities of God in the hope that she will follow into His green pasture of love.

So off we go with the stinking sheepskin seat covers. Thankfully, she has the canvas top down today so I can breathe a little fresh air.

> *"'For this is what the Sovereign Lord says: I myself will search for my sheep and look after them. As a shepherd looks after his scattered flock when he is with them, so will I look after my sheep....*
> *"'You my sheep, the sheep of my pasture, are people, and I am your God, declares the Sovereign Lord.'"*
> —Ezekiel 34:11–12, 31

*S*overeign Lord, search for, _____, and look after him/her. As a shepherd looks after his scattered flock when he is with them, please look after _____. Make _____
Your sheep, the sheep of Your pasture and be his/her God. I pray this in Jesus's name. Amen.

— ◆ ◆ ◆ —

Restoration Service

B lack mold tinged with olive green crept through the floorboards. The home contractor stated, "Lady, you have a real problem on your hands. The plumbing behind the shower has been leaking unnoticed for several months. The drywall needs to be torn out and the pipes repaired. It's not going to be cheap, but it will look like new once we sanitize it and rebuild the shower."

Yes, I thought, *I have a real problem on my hands.* This shower mess mimics my wild child's life. She has sin oozing out of her. It, too, has been accumulating for months, maybe years. The partying lifestyle needs to be torn out and the joy of her salvation restored.

I cannot do much, but the Holy Spirit can purify her. He holds the ability to sanitize her from the blackness of sin. He can make her wholesome again. Of course, the cost is not cheap, but the blood of Jesus Christ paid for the ultimate and eternal repair.

Anyway, I will hire the general contractor to rebuild my shower. Then I will implore the Holy Spirit to restore the joy of priceless salvation to my wild child. Of course, the Holy Spirit will do a perfect job. My only hope is that the contractor knows what he is doing. I do not want to call any other restoration service.

Create in me a pure heart, O God, and renew a steadfast spirit within me. Do not cast me from your presence or take your

Holy Spirit from me. Restore to me the joy of your salvation
and grant me a willing spirit, to sustain me.
—Psalm 51:10–12

O God, create in _____ a pure heart, and renew a
steadfast spirit within _____. Do not cast _____
from Your presence or take Your Holy Spirit from _____.
Restore to _____ the joy of Your salvation and grant him/
her a willing spirit to sustain him/her. In Jesus's name. Amen.

———————— ◆ ◆ ◆ ————————

Whispers of Mercy to My Wild Child

Dear Wild Child,

This will probably be hard for you to believe, but I understand
you completely. Even though we argue continuously and at times
cannot stand the sight of each other, I identify with your feelings of
frustration.

Why? Because your personality is like mine. I know—*horror!*
Moreover, it is true you are going to become more and more like me as
you age. Our similarity is the reason we do not always get along with
each other. We are too much alike. Words like *headstrong*, *stubborn*, and
short-fused describe us. Put us together and we combust.

My child, I have mercy for you because we are alike. However,
Christ gives you mercy because He understands no one can be perfect.
Christ's mercy sent Him to die on the Cross, so that we could obtain
mercy and righteousness from the Father.

Ask for the mercy of God—it is the only thing that can keep mule-
headed people like us from personality calamity—because I want you
to know, my precious wild child, someday you will most likely have a
child with the same spitting-image personality as ours. I know. *Horror*
of horrors!

205

> *O Lord, hear my prayer, listen to my cry for mercy; in your*
> *faithfulness and righteousness come to my relief. Do not bring*
> *your servant into judgment, for no one living is righteous*
> *before you.*
> —Psalm 143:1–2

O Lord, hear _____'s prayer. Listen to _____'s cry for mercy; in Your faithfulness and righteousness, and come to _____'s relief. Do not bring _____ into judgment, but have mercy, for no one living is righteous before You. In Jesus's name. Amen.

———————— ◆ ◆ ◆ ————————

17

Whispers of Encouragement

Infinity

The math gene skipped our family. We do not understand algebra, geometry, or calculus. We can balance our checkbooks, but anything beyond basic arithmetic skills is beyond us.

However, one element of mathematics I do understand—infinity. Infinity goes on forever without end. The only reason I can grasp this concept is that I have experienced it.

I am often discouraged about my child's problems. Yet somehow, God always provides a message of encouragement. It may be a song that will play on the radio; a Scripture that will resonant in my soul; a friend who will call to chat about and pray for my wild child. The ways the Lord speaks hope to me are endless. He offers me eternal encouragement as I struggle with never-ending episodes of wayward behavior from my child.

I may not comprehend algebra, and I certainly do not understand my child. Nonetheless, I do grasp that the Lord understands both my prodigal and me. *"Great is our Lord, and of great power: his understanding is infinite"* (Psalm 147:5 KJV). Thankfully, I do not have to solve algebraic equations *or* my wild child's self-made problems. God's infinite understanding equals eternal encouragement for both of

207

us. Because of this, I can pray and not be distracted by discouragement. I will ask God to multiply His demonstrations of love to both of us. Our family needs no more division, but, instead, the union of understanding and encouragement. I know God will add these to our home so we can find a balance in our relationships.

May our Lord Jesus Christ himself and God our Father, who loved us and by his grace gave us eternal encouragement and good hope, encourage your hearts and strengthen you in every good deed and word.
—2 Thessalonians 2:16–17

*O*h, Lord God, demonstrate Your love to _____. Allow _____ to experience Your love and grace. Grant _____ eternal encouragement and hope. Encourage _____'s heart and strengthen _____ in every good deed and word. In Your name. Amen.

◆ ◆ ◆

Gnashing of Teeth

My flesh and my heart may fail, but God is the strength of my heart and my portion forever.
—Psalm 73:26

My left jaw ached this morning from grinding my teeth as I slept. Remorse and unforgiveness plague me at night. *How did my child go so wrong? What did I lack in parenting skills? Why can't I fix her?*

I used to speculate what *"gnashing of teeth"* meant when I read, *"'And throw that worthless servant outside, into the darkness, where there will be weeping and gnashing of teeth'"* (Matthew 25:30). But now, I know. It is when someone thinks that they might have been able to do something to prevent the hell they are going through. When I read Matthew 25:30, I feel like that worthless servant. I believe I have failed my child. I think I have disappointed God. Somehow, I must be at fault for my daughter's poor life choices.

I gulp down an aspirin for the pain in my jaw. Then I gaze at the Bible verse taped to my vanity mirror: *"My flesh and my heart may fail, but God is the strength of my heart and my portion forever"* (Psalm 73:26).

Oh, yes! Even when despair and doubt strike my heart over the role I might have played in my daughter's destructive behaviors, God is still the strength that I must lean on. He is my portion forever, regardless of my own self-doubt.

*O*h God, truly I know what is meant by the term *gnashing of teeth*. Whether it is true or not, I feel responsibility for _____'s poor life choices. When remorse and self-accusation plague me and my heart fails with guilt, help me to remember that You are the strength of my heart and my portion forever. Help my wild child, _____, discover that You want to be the same for him/her too. In Jesus's name. Amen.

◆ ◆ ◆

Rock Hard

> *But encourage one another daily, as long as it is called Today,*
> *so that none of you may be hardened by sin's deceitfulness.*
> —Hebrews 3:13

The loud bass guitar thumps through the walls of our home. The screamed lyrics that I can barely understand chill my soul. Explicit sexual words slide together with profanity. The music rocks the house and hardens my child's heart. Each verse and chorus tempts my child further away from our family morals.

I walk upstairs and tap lightly on the bedroom door. No answer.

With my fist, I knock on the door as if in competition with the sounds emitting from the stereo. Suddenly, the door opens a crack.

"Yeah?"

"Hey, I thought you might want to grab something to eat," I say.

"Uh, where?"

"Oh, I don't know. What would you like?" I reply.

"Mexican."

"OK." I smile as the door closes.

Encourage and meet together—that I can do. I will meet with my child in a neutral place of activity. I will choose to encourage the positives and refrain from the negatives.

Let us not give up meeting together, as some are in the habit of doing, but let us encourage one another.
—Hebrews 10:25

The hard rock music stops. And thankfully, the walls stop shaking. *Oh, blessed quiet!*

As we head out the door, I rumple my child's hair in an act of fondness and parental encouragement. The lighthearted spontaneity produces a grin from both of us. The rock begins to soften.

*F*ather, teach me how to encourage and to connect with _____. Although I do not understand or accept the cultural influences in _____'s life, show me how to counteract the deceitful manipulation that can produce a hard heart. In Jesus's name. Amen.

————————— ◆ ◆ ◆ —————————

Dry Bones

My little boy used to love to break the turkey wishbone. We would pick the meat off the carcass, search for the wishbone, and set it on the windowsill to dry. Each day, he would ask, "Is it dry?"

Finally, the anticipated day would arrive, and the bone would be white and brittle. We each would hold an end, make a wish, and tug. The wishbone would snap! A big grin would spread across my son's face, "I won. Mine is longer; my wish will come true!"

Now it is my son who has spiritually dry bones. He roams in a secular world that shrivels his soul and sucks the truth of God's Word out of him. I witness the withering of hope, joy, and the promise of abundant life in my son.

Oh, but I know the Living Water. I do not wish; I pray. My God is able to breathe life into dry bones again. One day soon, I know my son will say with a big grin, "The Lord is good. I am no longer dry bones, Mom. Your prayers have come true."

He asked me, "Son of man, can these bones live?"
I said, "O Sovereign LORD, you alone know."
Then he said to me, "Prophesy to these bones and say to them, 'Dry bones, hear the word of the LORD! This is what the Sovereign LORD says to these bones: I will make breath enter you, and you will come to life. I will attach tendons to you and make flesh come upon you and cover you with skin; I will put breath in you, and you will come to life. Then you will know that I am the LORD.'"
—Ezekiel 37:3–6

Sovereign Lord, can the dry bones of _____ live? Only You know, O Sovereign Lord! Allow _____ to hear Your Words. Say to _____, "I will make breath enter you and you will come to life; then you, _____, will know that I am the Lord." I pray these words, in Jesus's name. Amen.

◆ ◆ ◆

Dungeons of Guilt

Invisible chains lock my daughter to her sin. She falsely believes she has no choice but to continue in her poor choices of lifestyle. Guilt plagues her thoughts. Accusations of wrongdoing ping-pong through her mind. Claustrophobic from her shame, she seeks solace in the very things that bind her.

My daughter states she feels like Eve trapped by her mistakes. Like Eve, she experiences the shame:

> *At that moment, their eyes were opened, and they suddenly felt shame at their nakedness. So they strung fig leaves together around their hips to cover themselves....*
>
> *Then the LORD God asked the woman, "How could you do such a thing?"*
>
> *"The serpent tricked me," she replied. "That's why I ate it."...*
>
> *So the LORD God banished Adam and his wife from the Garden of Eden, and he sent Adam out to cultivate the ground from which he had been made.*
> —Genesis 3:7, 13, 23 (NLT)

My wild child considers herself, like Eve, banished from God. My daughter's dungeon of guilt and shame bar her from seeing the truth of God's encouragement to her. He will not put her to shame, if only she would turn and seek Him. *"Now the Lord is the Spirit, and where the Spirit of the Lord is, there is freedom"* (2 Corinthians 3:17).

I encourage her, but my words fall with a thud against her discouragement. But I remain sure of the grace of my God. He will loose my daughter from the shame that binds this Eve-like child. My hope is in the Lord God Almighty. Hallelujah!

You know my folly, O God; my guilt is not hidden from you.
May those who hope in you not be disgraced because of me, O
Lord, the LORD Almighty; may those who seek you not be put
to shame because of me.
—Psalm 69:5–6

*D*ear God, You know _____'s folly. _____'s
guilt is not hidden from You. Help _____to hope
in You and not feel disgraced. O Lord, the Lord Almighty, may
_____ seek You. In Jesus's name. Amen.

◆ ◆ ◆

Bookworm

*S*he burst through the door with a smile spread across her face.
"I won, Mom! I won!"

The fifth-grade teacher had challenged the class to read books this
year. The student who read the most books by the end of the school
year would win a prize and, in addition, win the "prestigious job" of
sixth-grade class librarian.

My girl loved a challenge. In fifth grade, she became an avid
bookworm. She read for fun and read to learn.

In middle school, the Sunday School teacher issued a challenge:
whoever memorized the most Scripture verses would win a scholarship
to summer camp. Once again, my daughter rose up to conquer the task.
She memorized more than 50 verses that year and went to camp with
all expenses paid.

My girl still loves to read and acquire knowledge. Unfortunately,
my bookworm no longer devours the Bible. She has disconnected
herself from the church, the Bible, and her faith. She states, "It is
irrelevant, Mom. It's irrelevant!"

My bookworm needs the life instructions found in Scripture. Her life direction strays from God's truth. Her obnoxious behavior causes strife in every relationship within our home.

I know the memorized verses still reside somewhere deep inside her soul. I need to pray that they rise to the surface of her thoughts, touch her heart, and point her back to the Bible. This Book will be relevant every day of her life and point my bookworm to the only God who can give her the eternal endurance to face life's challenges.

For everything that was written in the past was written to teach us, so that through endurance and the encouragement of the Scriptures we might have hope.
—Romans 15:4

*D*ear God, everything that was written in the past was written to teach _____, so that through the endurance and the encouragement of the Scriptures _____ might have hope. In Jesus's name. Amen.

◆ ◆ ◆

Eternal Encouragement

It seems like an eternity since my child rebelled against me. Days turned into weeks, weeks into months, and now months into years. How long can I continue to wait when my heart longs for reconciliation—now?

No matter how I spend my time, thoughts of my child linger in the background. Faces, shadows, and words haunt my memories. It feels as if madness is creeping into my mind. Time seems to stop even as an unknown future stretches before. I cannot go on.

Yet God steps in to rescue me from complete hopelessness. He promises, *"Never will I leave you; never will I forsake you"* (Hebrews 13:5).

214

Jesus will always be by my side to strengthen and encourage me. I must remember it is only by the grace and love of Jesus that I am able to get out of bed in the morning. With His strength, I put one foot in front of the other as I go to work every day.

Eternal hope will sustain me. I will continue to wait.

May our Lord Jesus Christ himself and God our Father, who loved us and by his grace gave us eternal encouragement and good hope, encourage your hearts and strengthen you in every good deed and word.
—2 Thessalonians 2:16–17

*L*ord Jesus, I know it is only by Your love and grace that I have been able to wait for reconciliation with _____. I ask You to keep supplying me with eternal encouragement and hope. Strengthen me in word and deeds until _____ comes home by Your eternal grace. In Jesus's name. Amen.

————————— ◆ ◆ ◆ —————————

Happy Dance

My daughter's hair hangs limp around her face. The smell of greasy, dirty hair lingers after she walks out of the room. Her slovenly appearance displays the unhappiness inside of her. Depression dooms each day when she finally does crawl out of bed.

Laughter and life used to flow from her. She would dance around the room and clap her hands in joy over the tiny things that brought a smile to her face. Rarely did a frown or scowl darken her lively pixie face. She was a daughter filled with joy—she was my joy.

However, when her fiancé lost his life in a tragic motorcycle accident, grief overwhelmed her. Melancholy waylaid her hope in God. She refused to go to church. She resisted counseling. She has sought comfort in solitude.

215

At first, I understood. I waited. But after five years, she shows no signs of coming out of debilitating grief. I am becoming desperate as the depression continues to steal my daughter's joy and she sinks deeper into despair. Only my Jesus can rescue her. Only divine encouragement can coax her out of the despondency.

I want my dancing, clapping daughter back. I want to see her dance in happiness once again.

"Young women will dance and be happy, young men and old men will join in. I'll convert their weeping into laughter, lavishing comfort, invading their grief with joy."
—Jeremiah 31:13 (*The Message*)

*D*ear Father, allow _____ to dance and be happy again. Father, convert _____'s weeping into laughter. Lavish him/her with comfort and invade _____'s grief with joy. In Jesus's name. Amen.

———————— ◆ ◆ ◆ ————————

Shadow of Light

*S*hadow. The word usually holds a connotation of darkness. The term might be construed as a negative. The feeling of darkness frightens young and old people.

I remember watching a television show titled, *Dark Shadows*. Its make-believe characters of vampires and ghouls lived in darkness, and I felt drawn into the blackness of the make-believe world.

Now I watch my child hide in shadows of spiritual darkness. His obsession with the macabre alarms me. Why would a child raised to see the Light of the world—Jesus Christ—spin around to run into the devil's shadows?

I do not know, nor do I fathom why my wild child would choose to live in shadows of evil, instead of the goodness of the Light. It remains a mystery to me.

However, I do know even God has shadows. For Scripture states, *"He who dwells in the shelter of the Most High will rest in the shadow of the Almighty"* (Psalm 91:1). But His are not shadows of darkness, but shadows of light. This truth is supported in 1 John 1:5: *"This is the message we have heard from him and declare to you: God is light; in him there is no darkness at all."*

> *He who dwells in the shelter of the Most High will rest in the shadow of the Almighty. I will say of the LORD, "He is my refuge and my fortress, my God, in whom I trust."*
> —Psalm 91:1–2

*L*ord God, I pray _____ will dwell in the shelter of You, the Most High. I ask that _____ will learn to rest in the shadow of You, the Almighty. May my child, _____, say of You, "He is my refuge and my fortress, my God, in whom I trust." In Jesus's name. Amen.

———————— ◆ ◆ ◆ ————————

Whispers of Encouragement to My Wild Child

Dear Wild Child,

This may be hard for you to believe, but I have always wanted you to have the very best that this life can offer. When you were younger, I asked God to grow you into an independent adult. You are. I desired for you to find a godly spouse who would love you as much as I did. Well, that one is still on my prayer list. However, I am sure the Lord has the perfect plan for your life.

I want you to know that I think you are a wonderful person. I proudly call you my child. I would not trade you for any other person in the world. You are my child.

You are my child—my child who has inherited some good and bad traits from me. Yes, you are my wild child. I understand your strong will and rebellion. I struggle with those traits as well. I recognize the strengths of your character and the weaknesses, because I wrestle with the same things. Yes, you are my child—my wild child.

Let me encourage you to allow God to tame your vivacious vigor. Consent to putting on the yoke of Jesus: *"Wear my yoke—for it fits perfectly—and let me teach you;... and you shall find rest for your souls"* (Matthew 11:29 TLB). Permit His strength to guide and direct your life, because in Him you will discover a glorious inheritance and a mighty power that is beyond anything you can imagine.

My wild child, under the yoke of Jesus Christ, you will be gloriously wild. You will be independent in His strength. In addition, you will have the Perfect Partner, before and after any "perfect" spouse that may come along.

I pray also that the eyes of your heart may be enlightened in order that you may know the hope to which he has called you, the riches of his glorious inheritance in the saints, and his incomparably great power for us who believe. That power is like the working of his mighty strength.
—Ephesians 1:18–19

*L*ord Jesus, I pray that the eyes of _____'s heart may be enlightened in order to know the hope to which You have called him/her. Reveal to _____ the riches of Your glorious inheritance and Your incomparably great power if only _____ will believe. In Your name. Amen.

◆ ◆ ◆

18

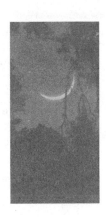

Whispers of Love

Fine Lines

There is a fine line between love and hate. I never thought I could hold such conflicting emotions over one person, let alone my child. My life changed forever the moment I gave birth to my son. I loved him more than life itself; without a thought, I would have given my life for him.

Then he grew up to be a man. Bitter battles wage between us. He cannot stand the sight of me. My heart drops when I hear the garage door open. He's home. Hostility hovers in the air. We both wait for the first challenge to come forth. Our mother-son relationship teeters on the edge of hate.

Although our love-hate relationship fluctuates on a moment-by-moment basis, God's love for both of us does not. Regardless of how we react to each other, God's response is pure love. Jesus did sacrifice His life for us because of His divine love—a love neither my wild child nor I can begin to fathom. It is love without end, and nothing can separate us from God's love—there are no fine lines.

For I am convinced that neither death nor life, neither angels nor demons, neither the present nor the future, nor any powers,

neither height nor depth, nor anything else in all creation, will be able to separate us from the love of God that is in Christ Jesus our Lord.
—Romans 8:38–39

*O*h Father, I am convinced that neither death nor life, neither angels nor demons, neither the present nor the future, nor any powers, neither height nor depth, nor anything else in all creation, will be able to separate _____ from Your love that is in Christ Jesus our Lord. Please help _____ to understand that nothing he/she does will change Your love for him/her. In Jesus's name. Amen.

———————— ◆ ◆ ◆ ————————

Papa's Arms

Strong men attract my daughter. She adores the lure of a manly man. Bad-boy types especially draw my little girl into illicit relationships. She flirts with married men. The allure of older men's arms causes my daughter to give herself freely to them. But the emotional high of the new relationship soon falls flat. Then she is out looking for the next guy to prove himself to her.

Everyone can see she is searching for the love of a father. She longs to be some man's little girl. My daughter grew up without a daddy in her life, and now she searches for that missing love. She's searching for love in all the wrong places.

If only she could realize that God's love is far better than a human father's love. He is the only Papa who can fill the love-hole in her empty heart. God is able to replace the temporary exhilaration men give her with permanent satisfaction. He will swing her up in the air and catch her. He will touch her spirit with everlasting love and end the eternal searching for a father's love.

This resurrection life you received from God is not a timid,

grave-tending life. It's adventurously expectant, greeting God with a childlike "What's next, Papa?" God's Spirit touches our spirits and confirms who we really are. We know who he is, and we know who we are: Father and children.
—Romans 8:15–16 (*The Message*)

*O*h, Father, allow _____ to experience the adventure of the resurrected life. Let _____ see You as her Papa. Touch _____'s heart and confirm who she truly is. Let _____ understand Your love as her heavenly Father. In Jesus's name. Amen.

———————— ◆ ◆ ◆ ————————

Hand Wash Only

Stubborn stains of sin linger in my child. He will not admit he is dirty and needs to repent. His pride refuses to acknowledge that imperfections might exist. Invincibility persists in his mind, although the facts dictate otherwise.

Funny, even as a little boy, he preferred being messy. He denied needing a bath even when caked with mud. However, back then I would simply pick him up and place him in the bubbly bath. The suds soaked off the grime. I would gently scrub any remaining stains with a washcloth held tightly in my hands. And in no time at all, out came a kid squeaky-clean from head to toe.

Now my kid needs a good hand washing—by Jesus. He needs to allow the nail-scarred hands of Christ to wash off the soil of stubborn sin that stains his soul. Only the Living Water can soak off the worldly grime. *"Though your sins are like scarlet, they shall be as white as snow; though they are red as crimson, they shall be like wool"* (Isaiah 1:18).

My child can be sparkling clean, if only he won't protest against the humble love of God.

221

When he came to Simon Peter, Peter said to him, "Lord, why are you going to wash my feet?"

Jesus replied, "You don't understand now why I am doing it; someday you will."

"No," Peter protested, "you will never wash my feet!"

Jesus replied, "But if I don't wash you, you won't belong to me."

Simon Peter exclaimed, "Then wash my hands and head as well, Lord, not just my feet!"

—John 13:6–9 (NLT)

*L*ord Jesus, I ask for my wild child, _____, to allow You to wash him/her clean. Help _____ to quit protesting Your authority over his/her life. Lord, I ask that _____ will exclaim, "Then wash my hands and head as well, Lord, not just my feet!" In Your cleansing name. Amen.

————————— ◆ ◆ ◆ —————————

Scarred

The bullet grazed across my son's cheek upward toward his forehead. The physician in the emergency room told my son that he was lucky to be alive. My wild child shrugged his shoulders and exited the sliding door. I could see revenge in the depths of his eyes framed by the purplish red slice that would soon become a scar for life.

I wish that was the only scar my child brandished. However, pockmarks from methamphetamines mix in with the freckles across his face. Tracks the size of pinpricks run up and down his inner arm from heroin needles. Hepatitis wastes his liver. Moreover, those are only the physical marrings.

The fire of hatred and revenge sears my son's soul. The years of drug abuse twists his thoughts. My child's own personality is lost in the torment of heroin highs and lows. Peace of mind eludes him as the potent drug deludes his senses.

Thankfully, no one, not even my addict child, is beyond redemption and healing. Jesus loved the scarred people of society. He hung on the Cross for every heroin addict. He died for those filled with hate. He rose from the grave, so that my wild child could experience the full extent of God's love through His nail-scarred hands.

But he was pierced for our transgressions, he was crushed for our iniquities; the punishment that brought us peace was upon him, and by his wounds we are healed.
—Isaiah 53:5

*L*ord Jesus, help _____ to realize that You were pierced for his/her transgressions. Grant _____ the understanding that You were crushed for his/her iniquities. The punishment that You took will bring peace to my wild child, _____. I ask that _____ be healed by Your wounds. Touch _____ with Your nail-scarred hands. In Your name. Amen.

———————— ◆ ◆ ◆ ————————

Double-Dipped

The cone towered with ice cream. My six-year-old licked it with her pink tongue. Suddenly, the strawberry swirl slithered down across the layer of maple nut. With a jerk, she attempted to salvage the double dipped cone, but to no avail. The swirl of strawberry smacked the hot pavement.

Steam arose from the asphalt gutter, while tears of disappointment ran down her freckled cheeks. My daughter's face crumpled into embarrassment, blaming herself for the accident.

"It's OK," I said. "You still have some ice cream."

"But, it's not a double dipped," she said with quivering lips.

It is still the same today, only now she is an adult. She always wants a double portion of every gratification of life. She grasps the pleasures for a moment, but then they slip into oblivion. She blames herself. Low self-esteem pushes my daughter down into the gutters of life. Hope of happiness eludes her because she desires a double delight.

Eventually, she will learn her yearnings will not prove powerful enough to bring her lasting joy. They will tumble to the ground and melt into disappointment, like her strawberry ice cream.

God promises to fulfill her desires, not only once, but with a double dip of His delight, if only she will look up from the gutters to the heavens.

Instead of their shame my people will receive a double portion, and instead of disgrace they will rejoice in their inheritance; and so they will inherit a double portion in their land, and everlasting joy will be theirs.
—Isaiah 61:7

*L*ord God, let _____ learn his/her lesson. Allow him/her to receive a double portion of Your Spirit with meekness and gentleness. Instead of disgrace, teach _____ to rejoice in his/her inheritance of faith. I ask for everlasting joy and delight to be the lesson that _____ learns from this experience. In Jesus's name. Amen.

◆ ◆ ◆

Ruses of Rascals

*Y*our son is so wonderful! I just wish my child would act more like yours. He's absolutely delightful."

"Thank you." I answer. Then I think to myself, *Are you talking about my kid? Uh, if you only knew what he thinks of you.*

Phoniness engulfs my son. He knows how to schmooze anyone and everyone. He uses his big brown eyes to soften people's hearts. His grin charms unsuspecting victims into granting his wishes. His disguise of love and affection for others disappears the moment they leave his presence. My child is a rascal.

He manipulates people with the ruse of his "Christianity." He masquerades as a godly guy. He looks fine on the outside, but inside he is like a sand spider. *Wham!* He draws people with false love and kindness in order for them to fulfill some part of his own selfish wants.

He sneers at people's gullibility, especially Christians. My son had better learn to adhere to the truth and the principles of Christianity. Jesus will not tolerate phoniness in His followers. My son had better wise up. Jesus knows how to change a rascal into a disciple, and it might just be with a *wham!*

> *Don't just pretend that you love others. Really love them. Hate what is wrong. Stand on the side of the good. Love each other with genuine affection, and take delight in honoring each other.*
> —Romans 12:9–10 (NLT)

*H*eavenly Father, help _____ to not pretend that he/she loves others. Aid _____ in truly loving. Teach _____ to hate what is wrong. Grant _____ the desire to stand on the side of good. Soften _____'s heart to love with genuine affection and to take delight in honoring others above himself/herself. In Jesus's name. Amen.

Nevertheless

Nevertheless. I cling to that word. No matter what my wild child does, *nevertheless* God holds her close to His heart. Yet it feels so hopeless. I wait and pray. I watch and wait. I watch and cry. Then I cry and pray again.

My child is like a speck of sand lost in a planet full of sinful behaviors. Her actions range from fibs to a felony conviction. The gamut of her wrongdoing extends beyond my conceivable imagination. The jury found her guilty. I begin to realize the reality of her sins when the judge slams down the gavel with the announcement of the sentence of prison time.

God formed the world, and He created my wild child. Although she is lost in the dust of self-destruction, God sees my daughter. He observes a speck of a girl sitting on a bench handcuffed. *Nevertheless,* He loves her.

I can only wait, watch, pray, and hold to this promise: *"This is how much God loved the world: He gave his Son, his one and only Son. And this is why: so that no one need be destroyed; by believing in him, anyone can have a whole and lasting life"* (John 3:16 *The Message*).

> *"This is what the LORD says, he who made the earth, the LORD who formed it and established it—the LORD is his name: 'Call to me and I will answer you and tell you great and unsearchable things you do not know.'"*
> —Jeremiah 33:2–3

*F*ather God, You made the earth; You formed it and established it. Your name is Lord. Say to my child, _____, "Call to me and I will answer you and tell you great and unsearchable things you do not know." Lord, grant _____ the understanding that You love him/her regardless of his/her sin. In Jesus's name. Amen.

◆ ◆ ◆

Cotton Candy

"Can I have just one more before we go?" my daughter would beg. "No, sweetie. You've had two and that's one too many." I would answer with a warm grin.

The sugar-high lasted for hours after leaving the amusement park. Sticky hands marred the windows of the van. My daughter licked her petite fingers and then twisted her pigtails around them. *She will definitely need a shampoo tonight,* I thought to myself.

Cotton candy, the silky angel hair delicacy, seduced her into a sugar glutton. She adored how it melted in her mouth. The sweetness of the treat was not overpowering, but gentle and nonfilling. She could eat it forever—a pleasure beyond compare.

Now it has all changed. My daughter is a young woman. She does not ask permission for anything. She streaks the car windows with fast food. She flatirons her hair; the braids are gone. She washes her hair every night to remove the smell of cigarettes. My daughter discovered a plethora of new pleasures. Adulthood presented a paradise of sensual sweets to her soul. She went from a "sugar high" to a "sin high." She is still sticky and messy, but with a different sort of indulgence.

Now I wait for her to mature. She is an adult physically, but a child emotionally and spiritually. My daughter will mature, eventually. She will mature into the knowledge that God loves her and that lasting pleasure comes in living a godly life. She will indulge herself in the sweet paradise of the joy of being in His presence.

You have made known to me the path of life; you will fill me with joy in your presence, with eternal pleasures at your right hand.
—Psalm 16:11

$\mathcal{L}$ord Jesus, make known to _____ the path of life; fill _____ with joy in Your presence, with eternal pleasures at Your right hand. In Your name, I pray. Amen.

———————— ◆ ◆ ◆ ————————

What Is the Point?

W*hat is the point? Why bother? How can I ever be close to God after what I have done?* These questions roll through my wild child's head. Whispers of Satan accuse her night and day. He lurks in the consequences of sin to remind her of the "crimes" she has committed against the Lord God.

Oh, but Jesus told us Satan is a liar: *"When he lies, he speaks his native language, for he is a liar and the father of lies"* (John 8:44). Satan lies to my daughter. Her rescue comes from Jesus, her Lord and Savior. He will lift her from the pit of darkness into which she has fallen and set her feet on high places bathed in the light of His love.

Satan may gloat over my wild child for a moment, but not forever!

"Now have come the salvation and the power and the kingdom of our God, and the authority of his Christ. For the accuser of our brothers, who accuses them before our God day and night, has been hurled down."
—Revelation 12:10

My daughter needs to lift her head and reach for His nail-scarred hand. She will arise in victory at the feet of Jesus and the Cross. Glory!

But as for me, I watch in hope for the LORD, I wait for God my Savior; my God will hear me. Do not gloat over me, my enemy!

Though I have fallen, I will rise. Though I sit in darkness, the
*L*ORD *will be my light.*
—Micah 7:7–8

*L*ord Jesus, show _____ how to watch in hope for You.
Teach _____ to say, "I wait for God my Savior; and my God
will hear me. Do not gloat over me my enemy." Show _____
that, through Your love, although he/she has fallen, he/she will rise.
Although _____ sits in darkness, let _____
understand You will be his/her light. In Your name, I pray. Amen.

◆ ◆ ◆

Whispers of Love to My Wild Child

Dear Wild Child,
    Do you remember when you first saw the gushing waterfall, Bridal
Veil Falls, in Yosemite National Park? You stood amazed as the water
thundered down over the rocks and into the crystal pool below. The
water was so loud that even when we shouted, we could barely hear
one another.
    We laughed as the mist drifted down upon us, but you wanted more.
You ran to the railing and the spray of droplets soaked you. Teardrops
of water ran down your face, puddling in the collar of your shirt. I knelt
as I attempted to wipe your wet, freckled face. It was impossible; so
instead, we held hands and twirled in the awesome grandeur of Bridal
Veil Falls, totally immersed in joy.
    Today, beloved child, I pray for you to experience the glory of
God in the same manner. He loves you and longs for you to immerse
yourself in His presence.

For this reason I kneel before the Father.... And I pray that
you... grasp how wide and long and high and deep is the love

229

of Christ, and to know this love that surpasses knowledge—
that you may be filled to the measure of all the fullness
of God.
—Ephesians 3:14, 17–19

Wild child, you seek thrills; God will thrill you with wonder. You seek wealth; His love is more valuable than anything this world can offer. You seek knowledge; Christ will fill you beyond measure with His knowledge.

My child, come twirl with me in the awesome grandeur and glory of Jesus Christ. I am on my knees with my hands held out to you.

Many waters cannot quench love; rivers cannot wash it away.
If one were to give all the wealth of his house for love, it would
be utterly scorned.
—Song of Songs 8:7

Father, many waters cannot quench Your love for _____, and rivers cannot wash it away. Your love is more precious than all the wealth of any house. Please allow _____ to understand and accept Your divine love. In Jesus's name. Amen.

——————— ◆ ◆ ◆ ———————

Scripture Index

New Hope® Publishers is a division of WMU®, an international organization that challenges Christian believers to understand and be radically involved in God's mission. For more information about WMU, go to www.wmu.com. More information about New Hope books may be found at www.newhopepublishers.com. New Hope books may be purchased at your local bookstore.

More Parenting Resources

from New Hope

Cracking the Parenting Code
6 Clues to Solving the Mystery of
Meeting Your Child's Needs
Laura Lee Heinsohn
ISBN 10: 1-59669-207-3
ISBN 13: 978-1-59669-207-7

Setting Up Stones
A Parent's Guide to
Making Your Home a Place of Worship
Martha and Greg Singleton
ISBN-10: 1-59669-219-7
ISBN-13: 978-1-59669-219-0

Mommy Pick-Me-Ups
Refreshing Stories to Lighten Your Load
Edna Ellison and Linda Gilden
ISBN-10: 1-59669-218-9
ISBN-13: 978-1-59669-218-3

The Mentoring Mom
11 Ways to Model Christ for Your Child
Jackie Kendall
ISBN-10: 1-59669-005-4
ISBN-13: 978-1-59669-005-9